Contemporary Issues in Land Use Planning

Edited by Seth Appiah-Opoku

Published in London, United Kingdom

Contemporary Issues in Land Use Planning
http://dx.doi.org/10.5772/intechopen.100668
Edited by Seth Appiah-Opoku

Contributors
Mohsen Armin, Dejene Tesema Bulti, Anteneh Lemmi Eshete, Mohammad Rahim Rahnama, Mehdi Sarparast, Maryam Niknejad, Issaka Kanton Osumanu

First published in London, United Kingdom, 2023 by IntechOpen
IntechOpen is the global imprint of INTECHOPEN LIMITED, registered in England and Wales, registration number: 11086078, 5 Princes Gate Court, London, SW7 2QJ, United Kingdom
Printed in Croatia

British Library Cataloguing-in-Publication Data
A catalogue record for this book is available from the British Library

Additional hard and PDF copies can be obtained from orders@intechopen.com

Contemporary Issues in Land Use Planning
Edited by Seth Appiah-Opoku
p. cm.

This title is part of the Sustainable Development Book Series, Volume 4
Topic: Urban Planning and Environmental Management
Series Editor: Usha Iyer-Raniga
Topic Editors: Christoph Lüthi and Rui Alexandre Castanho

Print ISBN 978-1-80356-236-0
Online ISBN 978-1-80356-237-7
eBook (PDF) ISBN 978-1-80356-238-4
ISSN 2753-6580

IntechOpen Book Series

Sustainable Development

Volume 4

Aims and Scope of the Series

Transforming our World: the 2030 Agenda for Sustainable Development endorsed by United Nations and 193 Member States, came into effect on Jan 1, 2016, to guide decision making and actions to the year 2030 and beyond. Central to this Agenda are 17 Goals, 169 associated targets and over 230 indicators that are reviewed annually. The vision envisaged in the implementation of the SDGs is centered on the five Ps: People, Planet, Prosperity, Peace and Partnership. This call for renewed focused efforts ensure we have a safe and healthy planet for current and future generations.

This Series focuses on covering research and applied research involving the five Ps through the following topics:

1. Sustainable Economy and Fair Society that relates to SDG 1 on No Poverty, SDG 2 on Zero Hunger, SDG 8 on Decent Work and Economic Growth, SDG 10 on Reduced Inequalities, SDG 12 on Responsible Consumption and Production, and SDG 17 Partnership for the Goals

2. Health and Wellbeing focusing on SDG 3 on Good Health and Wellbeing and SDG 6 on Clean Water and Sanitation

3. Inclusivity and Social Equality involving SDG 4 on Quality Education, SDG 5 on Gender Equality, and SDG 16 on Peace, Justice and Strong Institutions

4. Climate Change and Environmental Sustainability comprising SDG 13 on Climate Action, SDG 14 on Life Below Water, and SDG 15 on Life on Land

5. Urban Planning and Environmental Management embracing SDG 7 on Affordable Clean Energy, SDG 9 on Industry, Innovation and Infrastructure, and SDG 11 on Sustainable Cities and Communities.

The series also seeks to support the use of cross cutting SDGs, as many of the goals listed above, targets and indicators are all interconnected to impact our lives and the decisions we make on a daily basis, making them impossible to tie to a single topic.

Meet the Series Editor

Usha Iyer-Raniga is a professor in the School of Property and Construction Management at RMIT University. Usha co-leads the One Planet Network's Sustainable Buildings and Construction Programme (SBC), a United Nations 10 Year Framework of Programmes on Sustainable Consumption and Production (UN 10FYP SCP) aligned with Sustainable Development Goal 12. The work also directly impacts SDG 11 on Sustainable Cities and Communities. She completed her undergraduate degree as an architect before obtaining her Masters degree from Canada and her Doctorate in Australia. Usha has been a keynote speaker as well as an invited speaker at national and international conferences, seminars and workshops. Her teaching experience includes teaching in Asian countries. She has advised Austrade, APEC, national, state and local governments. She serves as a reviewer and a member of the scientific committee for national and international refereed journals and refereed conferences. She is on the editorial board for refereed journals and has worked on Special Issues. Usha has served and continues to serve on the Boards of several not-for-profit organisations and she has also served as panel judge for a number of awards including the Premiers Sustainability Award in Victoria and the International Green Gown Awards. Usha has published over 100 publications, including research and consulting reports. Her publications cover a wide range of scientific and technical research publications that include edited books, book chapters, refereed journals, refereed conference papers and reports for local, state and federal government clients. She has also produced podcasts for various organisations and participated in media interviews. She has received state, national and international funding worth over USD $25 million. Usha has been awarded the Quarterly Franklin Membership by London Journals Press (UK). Her biography has been included in the Marquis Who's Who in the World® 2018, 2016 (33rd Edition), along with approximately 55,000 of the most accomplished men and women from around the world, including luminaries as U.N. Secretary-General Ban Ki-moon. In 2017, Usha was awarded the Marquis Who's Who Lifetime Achiever Award.

Meet the Volume Editor

Seth Appiah-Opoku is a Professor of Geography and teaches Urban Planning and Analysis, Land Use Regulation, World Regional Geography, and a field studies in Africa course. He is a member of the American Institute of Certified Planners and has contributed questions to the AICP exam. He is the author of two books and has edited four others. He has served on the international editorial board of the *Journal of Environmental Impact Assessment* since 2003 and has published scholarly articles in several renowned journals. He served on a high-level technical advisory team that advised the government of Ghana on the preparation of a 40-year development plan for the country in 2015. He teaches at both the undergraduate and graduate levels, and has served on several thesis and dissertation committees.

Contents

Preface

Land use planning affects every aspect of life in all contemporary societies. It helps determine where and how homes, factories, parks, hospitals, schools, roads, sewers, and other essential services are located in our communities. Strong market forces as well as individual and societal values play a major role in decisions regarding types and intensity of land uses. Faced with complex land use planning problems around the globe, we turned to specialists who have successfully undertaken empirical studies and analysis of rural and urban planning problems to share their experiences in this book. The biographies of those whose chapters comprise this book indicate they are singularly qualified for this task.

Chapter 1 by Mohsen Armin discusses agricultural land preservation plans and laws in Iran. The chapter argues that deterrence is not an effective solution to agricultural land management problems; it is necessary to include incentive and punitive aspects in a comprehensive land management plan. The chapter goes on to suggest land monitoring and evaluation system and the granting of credit facilities to qualified people could help preserve agricultural lands in Iran.

Chapter 2 by Mohammad Rahim Rahnama discusses how a multiple-objective land allocation model (MOLA) is used to simulate the location of residential and industrial lands in Sarakh city, Iran. To a large extent, the result was in line with the projected development direction in the city's master plan. The chapter concludes that the MOLA model is a better approach to simulating urban growth due to its high speed, accuracy, and low-cost compared to traditional methods of preparing master plans in similar cities in developing countries.

Chapter 3 by Issaka Kanton Osumanu discusses the implementation and management of urban land use plans in Ghana. The chapter argues that towns and cities need land use plans to direct and promote their growth in an organized manner. Based on a systematic review of existing literature and personal observations, the chapter reveals that urban planning in Ghana has adopted a three-tier land use planning model that considers spatial planning at various sub-state levels. It concludes that urban land use plan implementation and management in the country are thwarted by slow, cumbersome, and unending land delivery processes, as well as weak public participation, obsolete land use policies and methods, and insufficient human and financial resources.

Chapter 4 by Dejene Tesema Bulti and Anteneh Lemmi Eshete discusses the effects of urbanization and the quantitative methods for analyzing urban expansion. The chapter argues that the choice of a particular method depends on several factors, making it difficult for users to make informed decisions. Given the importance of analyzing the spatiotemporal growth of built-up areas for sustainable urbanization, the chapter provides a good insight into the main features of the existing methods that are used by urban planners.

Finally, Chapter 5 by Mehdi Sarparast and Maryam Niknejad discusses the links between land use changes and policy decisions in northeastern Iran. The chapter argues that most of the land degradation in the region is the result of erroneous and unscientific policies that may be beneficial in the short term but have long-term negative impacts on human societies and the environment. A simple analytical framework is used to capture the driving forces of land use changes, pressures, state of affairs, responses, and impacts (DPSIR framework).

As pointed out in my previous edited volumes in this series, this book must be seen as a wide brush stroke pointing the way to matters regarding contemporary land use planning problems because the case studies are limited in scope and do not cover every important issue in the discipline. Nevertheless, it is insightful, thought-provoking, concise, and easy to understand. It is an important reference material on similar contemporary land use planning issues in the developing world.

Seth Appiah-Opoku, Ph.D., AICP
Professor,
Member, American Institute of Certified Planners,
Geography Department,
University of Alabama,
Tuscaloosa, AL, USA

Section 1

Rural Land Use Planning

Chapter 1

Agricultural Lands Preservation Plans and Laws in Iran: A Case Study

Mohsen Armin

Abstract

In this chapter, laws and plans for the preservation of agricultural lands in Iran were expressed. For this purpose, electronic search of research background in the SID, Iran Doc and Sivilica was done. Results show that immediately after the Land Reform in Iran in 1971, Plans and laws including Agricultural Joint Stock Companies, Production Cooperatives Companies and so on have been implemented. The chapter argues that the approach of prevention and deterrence of land use change alone cannot be considered an effective solution for agricultural land management, and it is necessary to pay attention to the incentive and punitive aspects of careful land management and prepare a comprehensive land management document based on it. In addition to maintaining good quality agricultural land, the needs of other sectors such as industry and nature tourism to be properly addressed. Evidence show that in Iran, despite many laws and numerous plans, the process of changing the use of agricultural land has not been effectively controlled. Therefore, various suggestions such as setting up a land monitoring and evaluation system, granting facilities for the purchase of agricultural land to qualified people and so on are regularly presented by academic societies and executive experts.

Keywords: agricultural lands, preservation, development plans, laws, Iran

1. Introduction

Information on Land Use and Land Cover (LULC) and the possibility of optimal use of them is essential for the selection, planning and implementation of land use plans in order to meet the growing demands of basic human needs and social welfare. Planning for development in any country should be done according to the needs and conditions and requirements of that country and the capacities and needs of each country require a specific type of planning. This information will help us monitor land use change due to changing population demand, which is essential for coordinated action at the national and international levels. In general, the preservation of agricultural land use in Iran for various reasons, including insisting on the use of one-dimensional deterrent approaches, vague and incomplete laws, lack of land management plans, lack of specialized manpower and very high prices for residential land and industry did not have the necessary efficiency. In this chapter, first, issues related to the background of agriculture, the extent of agricultural lands, the position of the agricultural industry, the main planning approaches in the field of agriculture, the problems of the agricultural sector and the situation of land degradation in Iran were presented. Then, different approaches and views on the importance and preservation of agricultural lands and the factors of their change of use and laws and plans for the preservation of agricultural lands and prevention of their change of use in Iran were expressed.

2. Methodology

Electronic search of research background using key terms of agriculture in Iran in terms of history, size and place in the economy as well as plans and laws for the preservation of agricultural lands in Iran in the Scientific Database of University Jihad (SID, https://www.sid.ir), Iran Doc (https://irandoc.ac.ir/) and Sivilica (www.CIVILICA.com) was done. Inclusion criteria were (a) studies published without time limit, (b) papers related to various aspects of the agricultural issue in Iran, and (c) access to the full text of the papers. The result of this search was the acquisition of several papers which were reviewed due to their inclusion criteria.

3. Background of agriculture in Iran

Iran is one of the first countries in the world where agriculture and civilization began and early humans for the first time on the Iranian Plateau began to cultivate and raise livestock. It is also said that the migration of the Aryans, unlike the famous pastoral migration, was not in search of new pastures, but in peasant migration and in search of better land for agriculture. The global registration of an aqueduct-based agricultural system as an important agricultural system has made Iran the first and only country with a registered heritage in the Middle East and ECO member countries.

In the first century BC, the Persians planted all the fruit trees grown in Greece (except olives). With the invasion of Alexander, the Macedonian (336–323 BC) Iranian agriculture declined and many farms were destroyed, and this situation continued until the Sassanid dynasty came to power (224 AD). The Sassanids rebuilt aqueducts and encouraged and expanded agriculture, horticulture and animal husbandry. Agriculture with privileged irrigation systems was the basis of the Sassanid imperial economy and its share in the national economy was more than commercial. After the Sassanids until the Mongol invasion (1219–1256 AD), Iranian agriculture periodically stagnated.

During the reign of Pahlavi, along with industrial developments, programs were implemented in the agricultural and livestock sectors of Iran. Traditional Iranian agriculture was mechanized for the first time and the principles of work were introduced into it. However, the mechanization of agriculture was not universal and occurred only in certain places. Irrigation networks, dams and water containment helped boost agriculture throughout the country.

During the reign of Mohammad Reza Pahlavi, the Shah decided to make changes, especially in the field of agriculture, by implementing Land Reforms (1961 AD). Based on this plan, it was decided to make fundamental changes in the amount and manner of land ownership, especially agricultural lands and pastures.

Land Reform, or the abolition of the landlord-slave system, brought about fundamental changes in the way land was owned, especially agricultural land, in order to increase the general productivity of society. In this plan, the ownership of agricultural land from feudal lords or large landowners to smallholders and its redistribution among farmers, with the approval of the Land Reform Law and then its amendment laws and regulations, the law of division and sale of leased land to tenant farmers and the law of annexation eight Article to the Land Reform regulations was done in three stages. Land Reform was the first principle of the charter of the revolution of the Shah and the people.

In fact, in the period before the Land Reform, agricultural lands in Iran were cultivated collectively and in the form of rural communities, and the product obtained belonged to them, but gradually with the formation and growth of productive forces, the field of ownership collective and tribal groups have been eroded and individual and private property has been formed over time.

After the 1979 revolution in Iran and the coming to power of the new government, the process of Land Reform underwent a general change. On July 12, 1984, the Guardian Council of the Islamic Republic of Iran declared the implementation of Land Reform laws contrary to Islamic law, and the process of Land Reform was stopped altogether. Seven years later, on May 23, 1991, the Expediency Discernment Council legalized the continuation of the Land Reform process, and finally, on January 23, 2003, the Land Reform Council designated the gardens assigned to Articles 27 and 28 of the Land Reform regulations to be approved by the Expediency Discernment Council and the process of assigning the remaining Land Reform tasks resumed. Currently, the Land Affairs Organization is the sole custodian of the remaining Land Reform affairs in the country, and the Land Reform experts based in the organization's land management and development office are the last in charge of Land Reform in Iran [1].

4. Extent of agricultural lands in Iran

With an area of 165 million hectares and the benefit of various climates and despite the limitations of water and soil, Iran is one of the agricultural hubs of the world. According to a report in 2020 and according to FAO information, Iran has been one of the ten largest countries in the world in the production of agricultural products. According to FAO experts, Iran has the ability to produce and meet the total domestic and neighboring countries' need for agricultural products and can also meet the needs of countries bordering the Persian Gulf. Iran's agriculture, however, is struggling to access water.

Of the total area of the country, about 23 million hectares (equivalent to 15% of the country's area), are prone to agricultural activities. Of this figure, about 18.7 million hectares are currently in the cycle of agricultural products and an average of 14.8 million hectares of agricultural land in the country is cultivated annually of which 5 million and 997 thousand hectares are irrigated and the rest are rainfed. The alluvial part or Basin of Sefidrood River in the north, Moghan plain in the northwest and the downstream plains of Karun, Dez and Karkheh rivers in Khuzestan province have a more fertile soil area than other agricultural areas in Iran. Most of the arable lands of Iran, respectively, are located in the provinces of Khuzestan, Khorasan Razavi, Fars, Kerman and Isfahan. **Table 1** shows the general view of the lands of Iran.

Title	Area (million hectares)	Percentage of total land	Percentage of agricultural land
The total area of the country	165	100	—
The land area of the country	153	92.7	—
Area of agricultural land	23	14	100
Land area in agricultural production cycle	18.7	11.3	81
Land area with agricultural development potential	4.3	2.6	19
Annual cultivated area	14.8	9	64

Table 1.
General view of the country's lands [2].

According to the population of the country (about 80 million people) and the area under cultivation of agricultural lands, the per capita of each land in the production cycle is shown in **Table 2**.

Figure 1 shows the irrigated and rainfed farmlands in Iran.

Figure 2 shows the Fallow and Cultivated Farmlands in Iran.

Figure 3 shows the Cultivated Farmlands by Products in Iran.

Agricultural lands and per capita	Hectares
Per capita of each Iranian of Lands in the agricultural production cycle	0.24
Per capita of each Iranian farmer of lands in the agricultural production cycle	4.1
Per capita of each Iranian of agricultural lands under cultivation	0.2
Per capita of each Iranian farmer of agricultural lands under cultivation	3.3
Per capita agricultural land in developing countries	0.7
Per capita agricultural land in developed countries	0.66

Table 2.
Per capita share of land and agricultural lands [2].

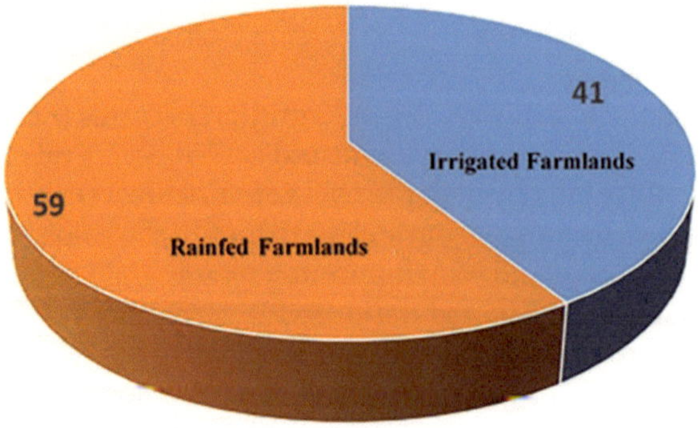

Figure 1.
Irrigated and Rainfed Farmlands (%) (2014) [3].

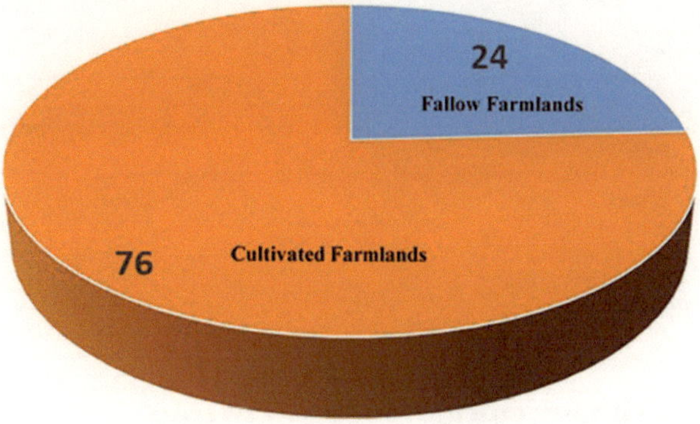

Figure 2.
Fallow and Cultivated Farmlands (%) (2014) [3].

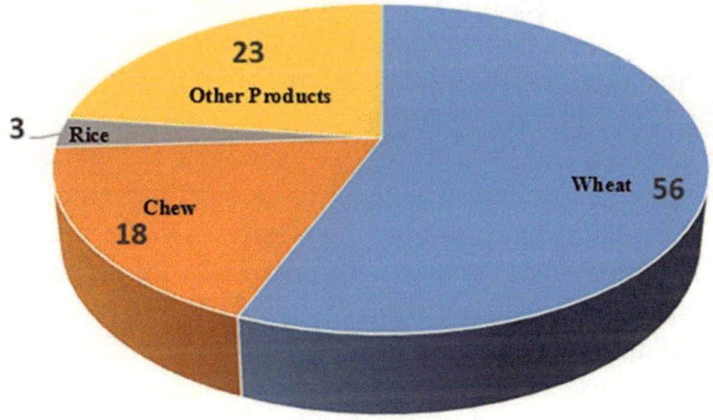

Figure 3.
Cultivated Farmlands by Products (%) (2011) [3].

Other crops, in percentage of cultivation, include alfalfa, tomatoes, vegetables, cucumbers, peas and beans, saffron, potatoes and onions.

Figure 4 shows the Farmlands and Garden and Nursery in Iran.

Table 3 shows the general view of Agricultural Lands of Iran.

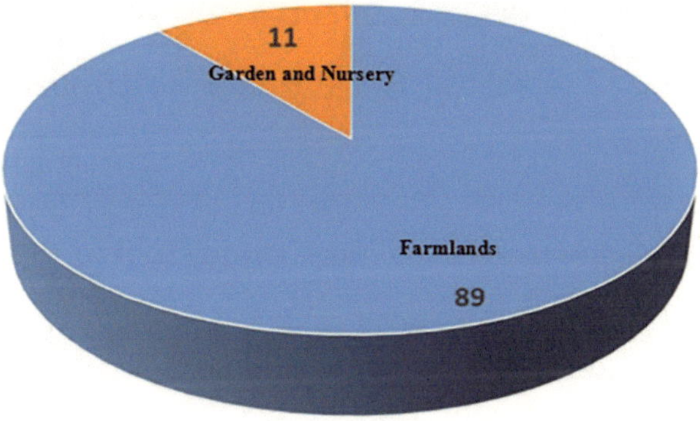

Figure 4.
Farmlands and Garden and Nursery (%) (2014) [3].

Agricultural Lands	Percentage
Follow Farmlands	53
Farmlands Irrigated	36
Garden and Nursery Follow	1
Follow Garden and Nursery	10

Table 3.
Agricultural Lands in Iran.

5. The position of the agricultural industry in Iran

The agricultural sector is one of the most important economic sectors in the country due to the provision of food needed by society, GDP and economic growth, which on the one hand has a high share in the added value of the country's economy and on the other hand, has a significant share in employment. Due to its extensive connections with other economic sectors, this sector can, with its growth, provide the ground for wealth production, market creation and currency generation, and the growth of industry and services sectors.

Agriculture in Iran is an important part, and the agricultural economy is a significant part of the country's economy. The share of labour force employed in the agricultural sector in relation to the total number of employees in the world is 26.5%, while this share in Iran is estimated at 17.6% [4]. The share of value added of the agricultural sector at fixed prices in the world is estimated at 3.5% and in Iran at 6% [3].

Iran's agricultural production has increased from 96.8 million tons in 2013 with a growth of 6.6% to more than 103 million tons in 2014. The value of exports of agricultural products and food industries increased from $ 5.6 billion in 2014 to $ 6.5 billion in 2015. Agricultural production in 2015 increased from 103 million tons to 112 million tons.

According to the statistics obtained from 117 million tons of agricultural products produced in Iran, 82 million tons of those agricultural products, 2.5 million tons of horticultural products, 13.7 million tons of livestock products and one million tons of other products have been reported. According to these statistics, nearly a quarter of agricultural production is lost due to the lack of Iranian agricultural industry.

The share of different agricultural sectors in the value added of this sector and the fixed price in Iran is as follows [5].

Figure 5 shows the Added value of various agricultural activities at a fixed price (2011–2015) in Iran.

6. The main approaches to agricultural planning in Iran

- Emphasis on economics and knowledge-based production based on educated human resources and the use of new technologies as the main factors of wealth creation.

- Economics based on high productivity of production factors, efficiency of distribution and application of knowledge in management.

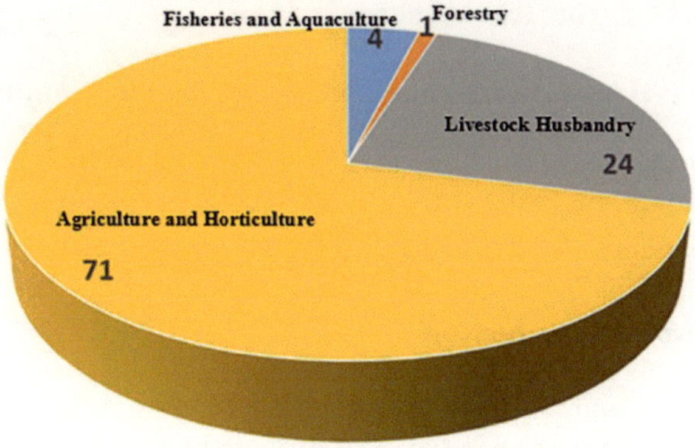

Figure 5.
Added value of various agricultural activities at a fixed price (2011–2015) [5].

- Effective relationship between science production process and product production and distribution process.
- Efficiency of research management and promotion of important requirements for the realization of agriculture with a knowledge-based economy approach.
- Demand-driven research, effective training and promotion of new technologies are the most important assets and capabilities for transformation in the agricultural sector.
- Specialized and motivated human resources, managers, experts and researchers and an extensive network of promotion and cooperation and participation of organizations and users in the country
- Development of applied research and transfer of technical knowledge and new technologies in order to maintain and use sustainable and optimal production resources
- Targeted support policies and business competitiveness and economic production.
- Optimal use of water and soil capacities in different regions with the aim of establishing and dispersing the population of the country
- Investment is the main factor of agricultural growth and plays a decisive role in the productivity of factors of production. Investment is an important and effective factor in the continuation of production, strengthening food security and sustainability.
- Insufficient investment causes a gradual increase in the cost prices of products and the loss of the comparative advantage of domestic production and the impossibility of competition in the global and regional markets.
- The need for cross-sectoral and national management in the water crisis.

7. Problems of the agricultural sector in Iran

7.1 Insufficient confidence in ensuring food security of the country

- Low self-sufficiency coefficient, especially in basic products
- Strong dependence of livestock and poultry industry on imported inputs

7.2 The main sources of production

- Limited water resources of the country and its quantitative and qualitative decline in many plains and imbalances in aquifers
- Insufficient investment and investment imbalance in the implementation of water supply projects, watershed management and construction of irrigation networks and equipment and renovation
- Lack of governance of agricultural water demand management
- Low irrigation efficiency
- Lack of adequate supply and adequate timing of inputs such as fertilizers, pesticides and seeds
- Lack of attention to the principles of soil preservation, surface soil erosion and reduced fertility
- Low productivity of resources and factors of production
- Continuation of the process of land use change, improper exploitation of forests and pastures and increase of degradation and desertification process

7.3 New technologies

- Weak mechanization in production, operation, processing, packaging and storage processes
- Weakness of information technology in producing accurate, coherent and timely statistics and information resources regarding basic resources and products
- Lack of comprehensive program guidance mechanisms and cultivation pattern
- Existence of high wastes, weakness of quality standards and technical criteria and standards in the production and supply of agricultural products

7.4 Cross-sectoral inconsistencies and economic policies

- Uncoordinated management of water and agriculture sectors

- Inconsistency of macro and sectoral policies
- Weak connection between programs, policies and policies of monetary, financial, banking, industry, foreign trade, transportation, higher education and research, etc. with the agricultural sector
- Low share of investment in value-added and lack of injection of financial resources through the public budget to the agricultural sector
- Sporadic production chain management, severe fluctuations in the input and product market
- Lack of transport infrastructure, storage and export terminals

7.5 Socio-economic development of rural and nomadic communities

- Structural weakness in the social security of producers and rural society
- Underdevelopment of villages and nomadic communities and lack of diversity of business activities in these areas
- Lack of knowledge about the social status of agriculture and the involuntary migration of young and creative forces from this sector
- Aging age of farmers and uncertainty about the future

7.6 Managing the public sector in the effective management of the agricultural sector

- Weakness of the system of education, promotion and applied and demand-oriented research, effective and applied and incomplete communication between the elements of the knowledge and information system and the inactivity of the private sector
- Weak public sector management in efficient management of the sector
- Lack of appropriate support mechanisms and lack of appropriate, sufficient and efficient development institutions in the sector

8. Situation of land degradation in Iran

Water and wind erosion processes are known as the most important processes that are active in areas of nearly 145 million hectares of the country with low to high intensity.

Due to the geomorphological conditions of Iran (prevailing arid and semi-arid climate and young geological unevenness along with the expansion of erosion-sensitive geological formations) naturally, the potential for soil erosion and degradation in Iran is high. But over the past few decades, the uneven development and inconsistency of regional plans with the natural potential of each region, along with climate fluctuations and successive droughts, have led to various crises such as dust storms, floods and mass movements. The result of these processes is land degradation and soil erosion in the areas of origin on the one hand and the problems caused by sedimentation in other places have reduced the overall soil fertility. About 43% of all organic carbon and more than 90% of all rare and nutrient elements such as phosphorus, nickel, manganese, iron and zinc are lost. Despite the occurrence of destruction phenomena, there is still no procedural unity in estimating the extent of land degradation. In the field of water erosion, a wide variety of figures have been reported in the field of soil degradation and erosion. In this regard, estimates made by researchers have shown numbers between 1 and 2.5 billion tons of soil erosion per year. According to some of them, Iran ranks first in the world and every billion tons of soil erosion is approximately equivalent to an average of 6 tons per hectare per year in the country.

In general, the following is said about the issue of land degradation in Iran:

- Land use change/land cover and land use management is proposed as the most important tool and solution to control soil degradation in Iran.

- Civil development and especially road construction and development activities with land use change/land cover are considered the most important factors in intensifying land degradation in Iran. So that since the 1990s, the role of human factors has been prevented much more than natural factors. Therefore, risk management and prevention should be sought by adopting a preventive approach instead of crisis management.

- In watershed management projects, vegetation restoration should play a pivotal role and structures should be created when necessary.

- The relationship between livestock and pasture should be considered, which is one of the factors of vegetation degradation and soil degradation.

- It is necessary to pay more serious attention to experts in land use management programs and land management and conservation agriculture, land degradation and soil erosion.

- So far, a small part of the whole country (one-fifth) has been included in watershed management programs. Due to the performance of these programs, by completing and eliminating the existing shortcomings in the field of structural operations, it is necessary to give more attention to the use of other methods such as bioengineering, water harvesting methods and the use of seasonal and temporary runoff.

- Many traditional and indigenous methods in all parts of Iran (such as Bandsar, Gorab, Khoshab and rainfall storage) can be considered as a support for participatory models of soil and water preservation and crop production in the country.

- Considering the importance and role of land degradation on food and social security, the issue of macro-management of natural resources and cultivation of sloping lands should be considered in the form of upstream laws, along with issues such as mining as a few examples of land cover/land use change be considered by managers and policymakers.

9. Different approaches and perspectives on the importance and preservation of agricultural lands in Iran

Due to the mismatch between the added value of agricultural and horticultural activities and the proceeds from the sale of land, the issue of how to use the land and its changes has always faced serious challenges for decision-makers, stakeholders and owners. Increasing demand for land use is affecting land allocation patterns and management practices [6, 7].

The issue of land use change and its extent is one of the main problems of the agricultural sector and one of the serious challenges facing sustainable agriculture identifying the factors affecting it is one of the important issues [8].

Changing agricultural land, due to its direct relationship with issues such as food security and environmental sustainability, has become one of the challenges facing humanity in the twenty-first century.

The intensity of land use change is such that according to the 2012 FAO report, between 1970 and 2009, the per capita arable land in the world decreased by 1.46% and in Iran by 2.554%.

Agricultural land use change plays an important role in changing global phenomena [9]. Although its dimensions vary from country to country, its consequences have raised more or less similar concerns in developed and especially developing countries.

With population growth and the industrialization of communities, significant changes in agricultural land use have occurred [10]. This issue is more important in developing countries due to poor management and disruption of political and economic structure [11].

In Iran, thousands of hectares of land are changed annually [12]. One of the serious problems of Iran's agriculture now is the change of agricultural land use after water shortage.

Justice statistics of different provinces show the increasing occurrence of land use change in the suburbs and cities of the country.

10. Different views on the importance of preserving agricultural lands

- Some believe that due to the low price of agricultural products, cheap import of agricultural products is possible. Given the general pessimism about the agricultural sector, these people believe that maintaining agricultural land use is not an important issue.

- Another group believes that the preservation of agricultural lands, given the need to maintain production capacity and the role of the agricultural sector in the economy, should be considered a local and national priority.

11. Perspectives on agricultural land preservation and land use change

There are different views on the preservation of agricultural land and its land use changes [13].

- Some believe that due to the importance of agricultural products, the country's lack of reliance on imports of products, etc., preventive measures should be taken to protect these lands (either as a punishment or as an incentive that eliminates the motivation to change land use).

- The second view, which is the approach of purposeful and systematic change of agricultural lands, believes that in contrast to deterrent methods and dealing with violators due to some necessities such as population growth, increasing urbanization, the need for tourism and the development of nature tourism industry, etc. In addition to the use of deterrent methods, land use change should be done systematically and purposefully (although this approach can be implemented according to article 12 of the Law on Agricultural Land Use Change).

12. Policy approaches for agricultural land preservation

- In the first approach, agricultural lands are allocated for different non-agricultural uses according to the policies and programs of each sector organization and without considering the perspective of preserving agricultural lands and efforts are being made to create minimum restrictions on the use of agricultural land for executive agencies.

- In the second approach, considering a large number of lost lands and the need to ensure food security, the axis of planning is considered the preservation of agricultural lands and the programs and projects of the executive organizations are formulated and implemented with this perspective and with minimal encroachment on agricultural lands.

In the second approach, it is well recognized that the change of use of each hectare of agricultural land means a direct and immediate dependence on foreign imports and a threat to food security.

The first view on the importance of agricultural land is consistent with the first approach to policy for the preservation of agricultural land and the second view is consistent with the second approach.

After explaining the general views and approaches to agricultural land conservation, the most important laws related to preventing the change of use of agricultural land in the country are discussed. This provides a basis for identifying general approaches to these laws [14].

13. Laws and plans for the preservation of agricultural lands and the prevention of their change of use in Iran

Preservation of agricultural lands as a platform for agricultural activities is one of the most important decision-making components in the field of agricultural development, because in all small and large communities, providing food security for current and future generations requires preserving existing agricultural lands for continuous and effective use, Therefore, its optimal use as a guarantee of human life is one of the important missions of policymakers and planners of sustainable agricultural development.

Today, the limitations caused by the destruction and inefficiency of agricultural lands in Iran are not a new issue and for many years, the focus of agricultural development policy makers has been on them, and they have always been looking for strategies and dealing with such bottlenecks. So that immediately after land Reform, agricultural development policymakers realized the negative consequences of land fragmentation and land use change and took measures to address this problem.

Preservation of agricultural lands is one of the issues in the framework of sustainable development. Agricultural land cannot be created and there is no operational method to restore modified agricultural land.

The most important methods of preservation and maintenance of agricultural and horticultural lands are to prevent land use change and micro-distribution of agricultural lands. In this regard, in Iran, projects such as the formation of Agricultural Joint Stock Companies, Production Cooperatives Companies, Agro-Industries Units, Common Production Units, Comprehensive Plan of Cadastre (demarcation) of agricultural lands, Agricultural Land Integration Projects, Concentrated Cultivation, Vicarious Cultivation and provided a Suitable Cultivation Pattern have been implemented [15].

13.1 Agricultural joint stock companies

Six years after the beginning of land Reform in Iran, the formation of agricultural joint stock companies in 1967 with the aim of increasing agricultural production and solving the problems caused by fragmentation and dispersion of agricultural land through land integration was considered.

13.2 Production cooperative companies

The law on the formation of production cooperatives companies was approved in 1970 to enable the integration of land and increase the yield and income of the villagers.

13.3 Agro-industries units

One of the forms of private capitalism in agriculture was the agro-industrial units, which were created from the very beginning with large capitals and on ready lands. The formation of agro-industries provided the basis for the formation of exploitation units based on the land capitalist system and contributed to the commercialization of agriculture in Iran.

13.4 Common production units

Common production units are the main collective agricultural units that were implemented in rural areas in 1980, following the approval of the amendment to the land transfer and rehabilitation bill. These cooperatives, in groups of 5–15 people, engage in common agricultural activities on the lands provided by the government.

13.5 Comprehensive plan of Cadastre (demarcation) of agricultural lands

In order to implement the Comprehensive Cadastre Law of the country approved by the Islamic Consultative Assembly in 2014 and also the circular of the Minister of Jihad for Agriculture, the Land Affairs Organization has put the plan to prepare a map of the Agricultural Land Cadastre on its agenda and the strategic document of the technical and executive system of this plan has been prepared, approved and implemented. This plan has been prepared in the form of vision and programs and policies of the Land Affairs Organization to improve and organize land management in the country. Therefore, one of the most central programs of the Land Affairs Organization is the implementation of the agricultural land Cadastre plan and the preparation of a spatial database of lands containing all layers of information related to land ownership and use. A cadastral map is a map that, in addition to geographical location, is prepared to show the location, ownership, use, and area of land in the study area.

13.6 Agricultural land integration projects

Land Integration, land reclamation and ownership in accordance with agricultural technology are being developed. In other words, it is a process in which dispersed lands are integrated to concentrate and preserve lands in areas that are inefficient or misused, barren lands or lands that have been damaged by production or natural and unnatural disasters. With the implementation of this project, suitable infrastructures such as roads between farms, irrigation and drainage canals and regular borders and activities such as leveling, creation of rectangular geometric plots, integration of scattered lands and scattered plots of farmers and additional operations such as construction of underground drains take place.

13.7 Concentrated cultivation

The purpose of Concentrated Cultivation is to produce similar crops in order to provide common agricultural services to farmers [16]. In this plan, by removing the borders and walls and hedges between agricultural parts, the parts are integrated, and a single crop is cultivated in it [17].

13.8 Vicarious cultivation Plan

Vicarious Cultivation is one of the localized and modified methods of land integration and monoculture. Problems such as inheritance and property boundaries and farmers' cash participation in different stages of production have been solved in this plan. In vicarious farming, the farmer receives services such as preparation, plowing, seed supply and planting, engineering and technical services, sunbathing, and harvesting and sales in return for providing land and after securing the income of the product, it settles the expenses of planting, holding and harvesting with the company.

13.9 Suitable cultivation pattern

The plan for the cultivation pattern of agricultural products has been prepared for several years and its basic plans have been determined and are currently in the final stages of registration. The final national plan for the cultivation pattern of agricultural products is to be implemented and operational in the near future in all provinces of the country [18].

Explain the approved laws regarding the preservation of agricultural land use in Iran.

A review of the experiences of different countries in relation to the preservation of agricultural lands shows that one of the most important tools needed to control the phenomenon is to use the law as a lever to be organized in the form of law and publicly.

Today, countries take strict care of agricultural land by adopting strict regulations prohibiting land use change and its strict implementation, as well as adopting incentive and deterrent methods.

Although various laws and regulations have been adopted in the field of preservation of property rights and prevention of land use change and illegal occupation of land in the Iranian legal system, in practice, facing this issue faces many social and economic legal problems.

13.10 Land reform law

Land Reform in Iran began with the approval of the Land Reform Law on December 10, 1971 and was implemented with a referendum on February 26, 1972. According to Note 2 of Article 15 of this law, a farmer who intended to sell his land, he could only do this deal with another farmer.

Of course, Note 23 of the Second Five-Year Plan (1955–1961) considered this restriction as a bureaucratic obstacle on the path of investment in agriculture and production and removed it.

However, due to the consequences of this the fragmentation of most parts, on July 25, 1964, a notification from the Land Affairs Organization stated that the implementation period of the second five-year plan law has ended, and therefore Note 2 of Article 15 of the law Land Reform is effective.

13.11 Law of agricultural development in agricultural poles

The Law on Agricultural Development in Agricultural Poles, approved on June 26, 1975, is the first law that explicitly emphasizes the preservation of agricultural lands. This law prohibits the conversion of the use of agricultural lands to non-agricultural, of course, within the agricultural poles. This law prohibits the separation and conversion of land use based on comprehensive urban, industrial and civil development plans and other plans that are deemed necessary. However, this law is limited to agricultural lands located in agricultural hubs.

13.12 Law on preservation of agricultural lands and gardens

The Law on Conservation of Agricultural Lands and Gardens was approved by the Islamic Consultative Assembly in 1995, and then the amendment law consisting of 8 articles was approved by the Islamic Consultative Assembly in 2006 and by the Guardian Council (Islamic Consultative Assembly Research Center, 2006). Article 1 of the Law on Preservation of Use of Agricultural Lands and Gardens states: In order to maintain the use of agricultural lands and gardens and their continuity and productivity, from the date of enactment of this law, changing the use of agricultural lands and gardens outside the legal limits of cities and towns is prohibited except in necessary cases.

This law was passed to prevent the change of use of all agricultural land. However, the many ambiguities and shortcomings in this law, including numerous exceptions and the limitation of its scope to agricultural lands outside the legal boundaries of cities and towns, have had little effect on the preservation of agricultural land.

13.13 Law on increasing the productivity of agriculture and natural resources

The law on increasing the productivity of the agricultural sector and natural resources, consisting of 35 articles and 36 notes, was approved by the Islamic Consultative Assembly in 2010. In order to implement the 20-year vision document of the country, the general policies of the system and the law of executive policies of

Article 44 of the Constitution, according to this law, programs, facilities, facilities to increase productivity and Reform production and consumption patterns in agriculture and natural resources were provided.

13.14 Law to prevent the fragmentation of agricultural lands and the creation of appropriate technical and economic parts

The law to prevent the fragmentation of agricultural lands and the creation of appropriate technical and economic parts consisting of 6 Articles and a Note was finally approved by the Islamic Consultative Assembly in 2006. According to this law, the Ministry of Jihad Agriculture is obliged to improve the productivity of production factors, optimal allocation of resources and prevent the separation and fragmentation of agricultural lands (including gardens, nurseries, irrigated and rainfed lands and their fallow) Within 6 months from the approval of this law, determine the technical and economic quorum of agricultural lands based on climatic conditions, cultivation pattern, mechanization criteria and quantity and quality of water and soil resources and submit it for approval. This law prohibits the division of agricultural lands into plots less than the specified quota, and the provision of any registration services, such as the issuance of a deed of ownership or separation, is not permitted.

13.15 Law on punishment for disrupting agriculture and animal husbandry

The Law on Punishing Disruption in Agriculture and Animal Husbandry in order to maintain the order of agriculture and prevent disruption in planting and holding and harvesting of agricultural and livestock products and thus preventing the closure or cessation of agriculture in the country on December 10, 1979 with 5 Articles approved. If land grabbing is considered as the occupation of lands, both governmental and non-governmental, by natural and legal persons, and the unjust, rental and illegal possession of land, it can be said that this law is one of the most obvious laws related to land grabbing.

Executive Regulations of the Law on the Assignment of Permanent and Barren Lands, which have been provided to farmers for temporary cultivation after the 1979 Revolution.

Article 10 of the Executive Regulations of the Law on Transfer of Barren and Permanent Lands, which was given to farmers for temporary cultivation after the revolution, states that any conversion of transferred lands to non-agricultural use and segregation, except in exceptional cases, was banned at the discretion and consent of the Ministry of Agriculture.

13.16 The law regulates part of the government's financial regulations

Article 110- The Ministry of Jihad for Agriculture was obliged sell the lands transferred by the land transfer boards to the farmers applying for purchase in cash and in installments, without exception and without any preconditions, at the maximum regional price at the time of transfer and deposit the proceeds to the general revenue account (with the General Treasury).

14. Conclusion

The chapter discusses restrictions on agricultural land degradation in Iran. It argues that it is not a new issue and for many years has been the focus of agricultural development policy makers who have always been looking for strategies to deal with bottlenecks. Immediately after the Land Reform in Iran in 1971, agricultural development policy makers realized the negative consequences of land fragmentation and land use change and implemented plans to address this problem. The chapter argues that the approach of prevention and deterrence of land use change alone cannot be considered an effective solution for agricultural land management and it is necessary to pay attention to the incentive and punitive aspects of careful land management and prepare a comprehensive land management document based on it, In addition to maintaining good quality agricultural land, the needs of other sectors such as industry and nature tourism to be properly addressed. It seems that in Iran, a large amount of high-quality agricultural lands has been easily lost due to the implementation of construction and development projects such as industrial towns, the expansion of cities and the transformation of villages into cities, and now the time has come to preserve these lands, the basis of work and planning for various organizations in the development and implementation of construction projects. Evidence shows that in Iran, despite many laws and numerous plans, the process of changing the use of agricultural land has not been effectively controlled. Therefore, in this context, various suggestions are regularly presented by academic societies and executive experts. Some of these suggestions include:

- Eliminating the reliance of law enforcement on financial resources caused by the complications of change of use

- Establishment of agricultural land evaluation system and preparation of relevant maps at a manageable scale and prohibition of any land use change in special agricultural lands (Class 1 and 2)

- Refraining from individualizing the decision regarding the granting of permission for change of use: since the pressure for change of use from the decision-making and influential authorities is usually high, therefore, while completely excluding high-quality lands from the subject to change of use, is necessary to avoid leaving any major decision-making to one person.

- Clarifying the process of applying for and issuing permits for change of use with the aim of improving public supervision: all supervisory organizations and non-governmental organizations supporting agricultural lands must have access to this system.

- Setting up a single window to submit requests for change of use and to inquire of organizations regarding the issuance or non-issuance of licenses.

- Capacity building in the judicial system to follow up cases of violations related to agricultural lands.

- Documentation of agricultural lands

- Setting up a land monitoring and evaluation system

- Granting facilities for the purchase of agricultural land to qualified people

Author details

Mohsen Armin
Faculty of Agriculture and Natural Resources, Natural Resources Engineering Department, Yasouj University, Yasouj, Iran

*Address all correspondence to: mohsenarmin2007@gmail.com

References

[1] Available from: https://fa.wikipedia.org/wiki/%DA%A9%D8%B4%D8%A7%D9%88%D8%B1%D8%B2%DB%8C_%D8%AF%D8%B1_%D8%A7%DB%8C%D8%B1%D8%A7%D9%86

[2] Agricultural Use Conservation. Perspectives of Policies and Plans of the Land Affairs Organization. 2014

[3] Statistics Center of Iran. Detailed Results of General Agricultural Census. 2014

[4] Statistics Center of Iran. Excerpts from Labor Force Survey Results. 2017

[5] Statistics Center of Iran. Added Value of Various Agricultural Activities at a Fixed Price (2011-2015). 2014

[6] Dieren W. Taking Nature into Account: A Report to the Club of Rome. New York: Springer Verlag; 1995

[7] IGBP/HDD. Land Use and Land Cover Change, Science/Research Plan. Geneva: Stockholm;

[8] Dehghan H, Azadeh F. Identifying factors affecting the preserve of agricultural land use to achieve sustainable agriculture. Journal of Agricultural Science and Sustainable Production. 2018;**28**(1):151-168

[9] Motiee Langroudi H, Rezvani MR, Kateb Azgomi Z. Economic effects of agricultural land use change on rural area (Dehestan of Licharaki Hasan-rood, Bandar Anzali). Journal of Research and Rural Planning. 2012;**1**(1):1-23

[10] Saadi H, Fereshteh AA. Factors affecting agricultural land use change in Hamadan rural areas. Journal Space Economy and Rural Development. 2018;7(2):211-226

[11] Long X, Ji X, Ulgiati S. Is urbanization eco-friendly? An energy and land use cross-country analysis. Energy Policy. 2017;**100**:387-396

[12] Boroumand M, Qajar Sepanloo M, Bahmaniar MA. The effect of land use change on some physical and chemical properties of soils (Case Study: Samskandeh Sari). Journal of Watershed Management. 2014;**5**(9):94-94

[13] Varmaziari H. Analysis of policies and approaches to agricultural land preservation. Office of Basic Studies, Parliament Research Center. 2015;**250**(14036):6-11

[14] Agricultural Land Conservation Plan. Parliament Research Center. 2016

[15] Shokati Amaghani M, Kalantari KH, Asadi A, Shabnali FH. An overview of the experiences of Iran and some Asian countries in maintaining agricultural land use. Scientific Journal of Land Management Extension. 2018;**6**(2):116-131

[16] Haghighat MS. Analysis of Land Integration and Crop Cultivation in Fars Province. Tehran: University of Tehran; 2012

[17] Shokati Amaghani M, Kalantari KH, Asadi A, Shabnali FH. Investigating the factors affecting the wisdom and dispersion of agricultural lands in East Azerbaijan province. Iranian Journal of Economic and Agricultural Research. 2018;**49**(3):487-508

[18] Keshavarz A. The national plan for the cultivation of agricultural products is being implemented. Iranian Students News Agency (ISNA). 2018

Chapter 2

Using Multi-Objective Land Allocation Model to Simulate Urban Growth: The Case of Sarakhs Border City in Iran

Mohammad Rahim Rahnama

Abstract

This chapter's purpose is to simulate urban growth of Sarakhs, using a Multi-Objective Land Allocation (MOLA) model. To achieve this goal, Landsat 7 and 8 and Sentinel 2A satellite images from 2003 to 2020, and 13 variables affecting the location of land uses with spatial decision model (SDM), multi-criteria evaluation (MCE), and MOLA model were used. Considering the increase in the city's population from 2020 to 2030 and the possibility of turning the city into a Free Economic Industrial Zone (FEIZ), about 322 hectares of land for residential use and 500 hectares for industrial use were estimated until 2030. By using MOLA model, the location of residential and industrial land use with a distance from agricultural lands was simulated in the west of the city. The result of the residential land use simulation is in line with the projected development direction of the City Master Plan to a large extent. But industrial land use is predicted in the vicinity of the Special Economic Zone (SEZ) in the west of the city. Therefore, the research results can be used in simulating of urban growth due to high speed, accuracy, and low-cost compared to traditional methods of preparing Master Plans in the Third World cities.

Keywords: border city, Master Plan, multi-criteria evaluation, multi-objective land allocation model, Sarakhs, spatial macro-model

1. Introduction

By 2030, 60% of the world's population—nearly 5 billion people—is expected to live in urban areas [1]. This increase in population will lead to urban sprawl and the loss of 1.8–2.5% of arable land, and 80% of this is in Africa and Asia. Given that more than 60% of the world's irrigated fields are located near urban areas, this indicates the potential land competition between agricultural and urban uses. Case studies show that high levels of urban development over the past three decades have led to the loss of agricultural land around cities [2]. In addition, rapid and unplanned urbanization has brought about dramatic changes in the urban-regional landscape [3], and the eradication of significant amounts of major agricultural land, including many environmentally sensitive areas, in suburban areas. To prevent unwanted changes in land use around cities and for the future physical guidance of cities, rapid population growth, and maintaining land use diversity, it is necessary to allocate land use [4]. Generally, Master Plans as a guide for public and private decision-makers are about the future physical development of the city, and the implementation of programs, policies, and projects [5]. These plans play an important role in regulating the future land use of cities [6]. Furthermore, Master Plans are traditional tools used by urban local governments, as planning tools for urban development [7].

Location of Master Plans is prepared more traditionally and semi-automatically through a combination of field studies and aerial photographs, topographic, and geological maps. Recently, GIS and TerrSet software have made it possible to use spatial decision-making and MCE and MOLA techniques with high speed and accuracy. By combining these models with Fuzzy-AHP techniques, not only the amount of land required but also the optimal location according to effective natural, social, and economic factors are provided. The results of Internet surveys have shown that so far, no research has been conducted on the choice of simultaneous location for two purposes (industrial and residential land uses) in the form of a Master Plan for cities. Studies have so far simulated most land use growth changes with different models of cellular automation and Markov chains, multilayer neural networks, etc. [2, 8], and some studies have predicted urban growth with the scenario; for example, in Kathmandu Valley Nepal, by the same models [9]. In addition, Hajehforooshniaa et al. [10] have zoned wildlife in Iran using MOLA model. Also, MCE and GIS models have been used to locate and prioritize landfills, retail centers, and solar energy farms [11].

The purpose of this study is to simulate the urban growth of Sarakhs border city on the border with Turkmenistan, in Northeastern Iran. It is actually the gateway to Central Asia countries with a population of more than 239,796,010 [12], and the gas capital of Iran, considering the possibility of turning Sarakhs into a FEIZ on the one hand and its strategic location on the other hand, urban growth needs to be guided in the form of a comprehensive plan with both residential and industrial goals with innovative methods.

2. Study area

The city of Sarakhs with a population of 42,179 (2016) is located at the zero point of the international border between Iran and Turkmenistan (**Figure 1**) [13]. It is located at 36°32′15.36″ N and 61°.09′40.49″ E [14]. The altitude of this city is 277 m above sea level. The Harirod river forms the borderline between the two countries. Similar to the Iranian Sarakhs, on the east side of the Harirod river, is the city of Sarakhs in Turkmenistan with a population of 9505 people (2009) [15]. In the scientific literature, when two cities are separated by an international border, they are referred to as twin cities. It shows their historical continuity. The two cities of Sarakhs were originally one. Until 1884, the Russians occupied the ancient Sarakhs of Iran, along with Marwa and Ashgabat, and annexed them to Russia [14]. The city of Sarakhs is the gateway to the Commonwealth of Independent States, which was formed in 1991 with the collapse of the former Soviet Union with nine members from the former republics [12]. Furthermore, Sarakhs was the gateway to the historic Silk Road to Iran [16].

Due to the strategic and geographical importance of Sarakhs city, in 1996, Sarakhs SEZ was established by Astan Quds Razavi (a non-governmental organization under

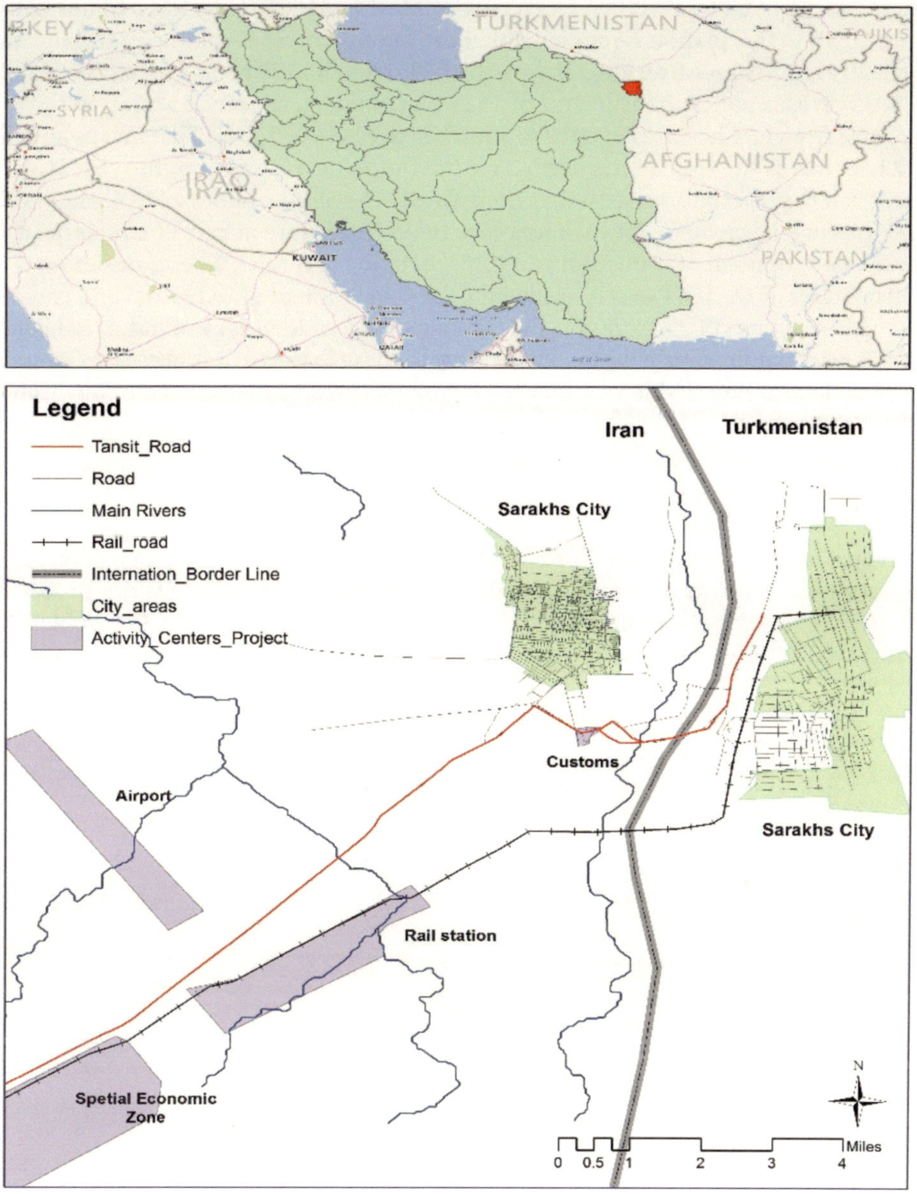

Figure 1.
Study area.

the supervision of the Iranian government) in an area of 4233 square hectares. Also, Sarakhs Diamond International Airport was put into operation in 1996 during the opening of the Mashhad-Sarakhs-Tajan railway [17]. Rail, customs, and terminals are other infrastructures for the development of the city and region. Sarakhs is also known as the gas capital of Iran because of the huge gas mines in the Khangiran region and the Khangiran refinery which is 40 km away from the city and was opened in 1984 and supplied gas to six provinces of the country [18]. The international and national situation of Sarakhs city caused the strategic and operational plan of Sarakhs city to be prepared by Ferdowsi University of Mashhad in 2016. Its forecast horizon is until 2030. In this plan, it is predicted that the population of Sarakhs city will increase from 2016 to 2030 with an annual growth of 2% from 42,179 people to 62,123 people in 2030. With a per capita land area of 162 square meters, the city is projected to increase from 684 hectares in 2020 to 1006 hectares in 2030 [14]. That means about 322 hectares of the land area is needed for the future development of the city. It is also predicted that if economic activities flourish and the SEZ becomes a FEIZ, about 6786 new jobs will be created. For each new job, about 735 square meters of land is needed for the development of industrial and transportation activities. Therefore, about 500 hectares of the land area is needed for the development of industrial and commercial activities [19]. As a result, the location of the residential and industrial land uses is essential for future development. Due to these features, it is necessary to use an SDM to determine suitable locations for future industrial activities and urban growth.

3. Materials and methods

The outline of the research flowchart is shown in **Figure 2**. The research process began with a literature review and proceeded in the following stages: (1) Pre-processing stage, (2) Using the spatial decision model, (3) MCE technique, (4) MOLA problems, and (5) Validation of the results of the simulation with the Master Plan of the Sarakhs and SEZ.

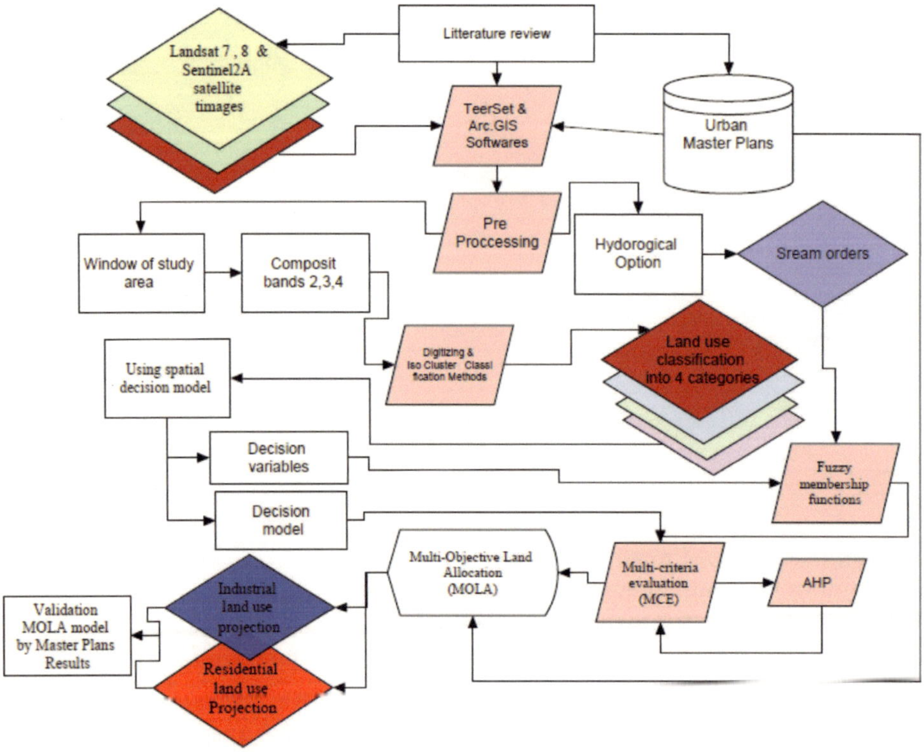

Figure 2.
Research flowchart.

3.1 Pre-processing stage

As can be seen in **Figure 2**, simulating urban growth is a complex and lengthy process. The diagram shows two parallel paths for research. (1) Downloading satellite images, Landsat 7 and 8 images through the USGS database for 2003 and 2020 [20] and Sentinel 2A images (2020) from the European Space Agency database [21]. (2) Studying the Master Plans prepared for the city of Sarakhs. In the end, these two paths are connected. The population forecast results of the Master Plan for the period of 2020–2030 have been used to allocate the land needed for residential and industrial land uses. In addition, the road map of the urban area was downloaded from the BBIKE site [22] and the DEM of the area's study was also downloaded from the USGS database. Also, using the hydrological option in ArcGIS software, river paths were created. The location of major industrial activities, such as train terminals, airports, special economic zone, customs, transit roads, were identified as separate layers. After that, the land uses were classified into four categories using the IsoCluster technique with TerrSet software. Due to the fact that in the SDM, each land use layer should be separated, by using the re-class command, the layer of the studied variables (13 variables) was separated in the form of a Boolean score (0 and 1). Finally, all land use layers that had been converted to raster format were re-evaluated with a distance command in TerrSet software (**Figures 3** and **4**).

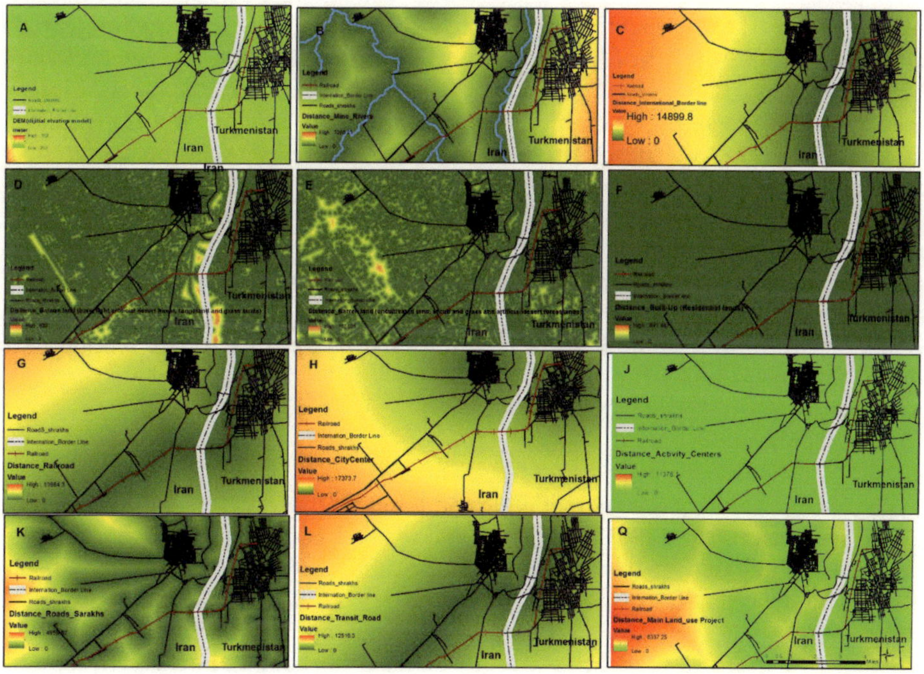

Figure 3.
Special, constraint and common driving variables: A = DEM, B = distance from main rivers, C = distance from international border, D = distance from bare land (bare, light artificial desert forest, rangeland and grass lands), E = distance from barren land (uncultivated land, shrub and grass lands), F = distance from built-up (residential and industrial lands), G = distance from railroad, H = distance from city center, J = distance from activity centers, K = distance from road—Sarakhs, L = distance from transit road, Q = distance from main land use projects.

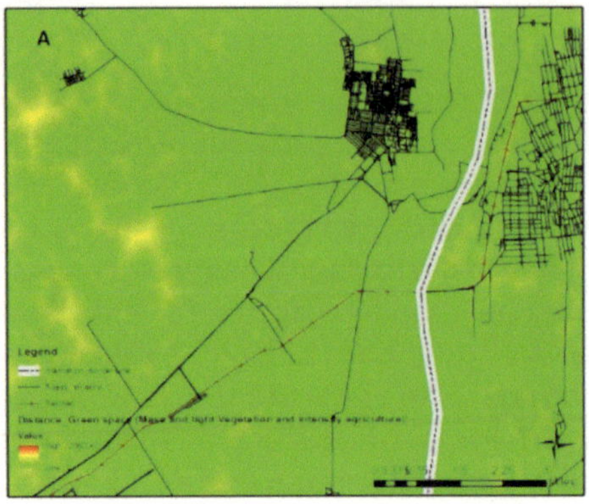

Figure 4.
Constrain variable: Distance_Green space (mass and light vegetation and intensity agriculture).

3.2 Using SDM

SDM is a graphical decision-support environment that can solve complex resource allocation decisions. This model uses the language and logic created around the decision support tools of the TerrSet system, including the development of effective factors and constraints with tools such as Fuzzy and Re-class, a combination of factors to produce appropriate maps with the MCE tool, and its combination by MOLA tool [23]. Due to the fact that this research had two objectives of locating residential and industrial land uses, the SDM was first called in TerrSet software. Then, 13 variables were entered into its environment through the decision variable menu, which included three categories of variables: (1) constraint, (2) common, and (3) special variables (**Figures 3–5**). These variables were selected from the decision operation menu using the fuzzy operation technique to fuzzy the value of the variables. Given that there are three membership functions in the fuzzy technique (monotonically increasing, monotonically decreasing, and symmetric). Based on the characteristics of each of the indicators, the functions appropriate to them were selected. Each of these functions can be calculated in three modes: (1) Sigmoida, (2) J-shape, and (3) Linear. According to the nature of the research variables, proportional functions (three fuzzy membership functions) were selected.

3.3 MCE technique

The MCE in spatial decision modeling combines multiple factors into one appropriate objective or map. At MCE, an attempt is made to combine a set of factors to achieve a single composite basis for decision-making according to a specific goal [10]. To use MCE operations in a spatial decision model, variables, factors, or goals and constraints must be connected to the MCE operator. One of the MCE parameters is the Tradeoff option. The weighting style or the resulting balance between the two desirable but incompatible characteristics is the degree to which one variable can compensate for the other. For example, with a full swap, a variable location with a high value can compensate for other low-value variables.

Another feature of MCE is the use of the AHP technique. AHP developed by Saati in the late 1970s is one of the multi-criteria decision-making methods. AHP breaks down a complex decision issue at different hierarchical levels. The weight of each criterion and

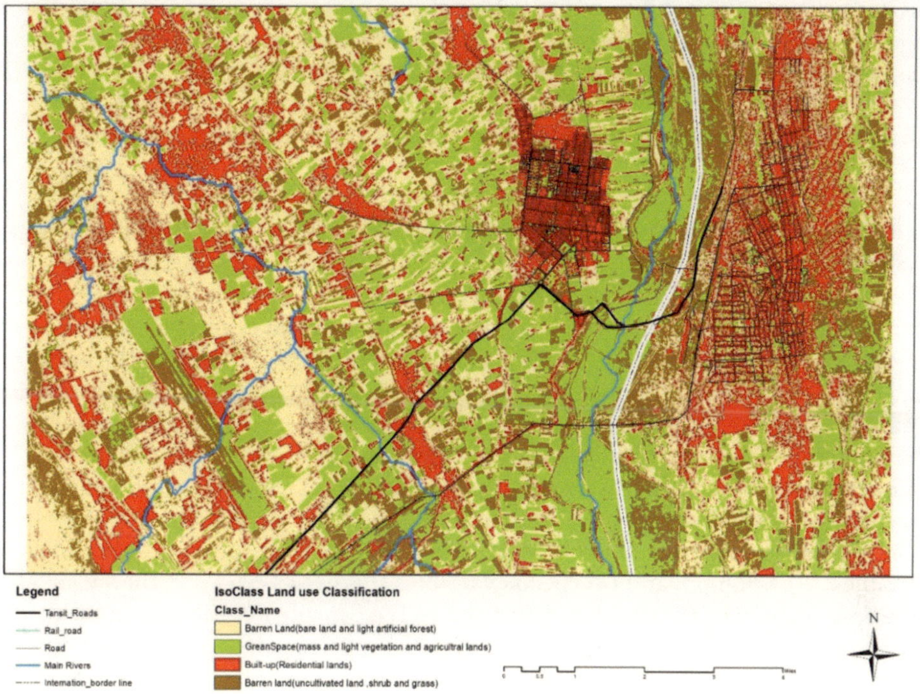

Figure 5.
Distribution of land uses in the study area in 2020.

its alternative is judged in pairwise comparisons and priorities are calculated by them [24]. In this study, after fuzzy (standardization), with the AHP technique, the variables were weighed in pairs (relative weight range from 1 to 9), based on the Saati table, and ultimately, the relative weight of the variables was determined. Furthermore, the indicators were combined by a multi-criteria evaluator. Then, the medium decision risk/no tradeoff option was calculated. Finally, the weighted variables were combined [10].

3.4 MOLA problems

This model provides a way to solve multi-objective land allocation problems for cases with conflicting goals. It determines a compromise solution that seeks to maximize the suitability of land for each purpose according to the weight allocated to them [10]. The user can specify either the required area or the maximum budget required to solve the allocation problem. There are options for forcing cohesion and compression [25]. In this research, the required area of residential and industrial land uses is 322 and 500 hectares, respectively. The option of continuity and compactness has been used due to being multi-purpose to locate the future development of Sarakhs city in the future horizon of 2030.

3.5 Validation of the results of the simulation with the Master Plan of the Sarakhs and SEZ

At this stage, the results of the MOLA model were compared with the proposed location of the Sarakhs and SEZ Master Plan through coverage alignment in TerrSet and GIS software. The ability and accuracy of the model were measured in determining the direction of development and guiding and managing the planned growth of the city. The research process can be seen in **Figure 2**.

3.6 Driving factors affecting the location of the future development of Sarakhs City

Identifying and selecting variables affecting the location of residential and industrial land uses in Sarakhs includes a wide range of different variables and hypotheses. These variables should have the following characteristics, in order to achieve sustainable environmental development: (1) Agricultural lands and vegetation should be preserved. (2) The proposed residential land use should not be far from the built-up area of the main city and should be connected to it. (3) Residential and industrial locations should not be on agricultural lands along the riverbed. (4) This land uses should not be at risk of river flooding. (5) They should be located on wastelands and near roads. These hypotheses are the most important features that distinguish this research from other research. In this study, according to the above hypotheses, 13 variables were selected, which were divided into three categories: (1) constraint variables, (2) common, and (3) special variables (**Figures 3–5**). First, the variables were re-evaluated by the distance command in TerrSet software. The status of these variables was determined in **Figures 3** and **4**. As can be seen in **Figures 3** and **4**, the value of the cells in raster maps increases with the distance from the variables.

4. Research findings

4.1 Land use classification of the study area

To predict a proper place for the future development of the city, both residential and industrial, it is necessary to study an area larger than the current state of the city (the current state of the city was 684 hectares in 2020). For this purpose, satellite images of Sentinel 2A were used [21]. Then, the land uses were classified into four classes using the IsoCluster technique with TerrSet software. The result is depicted in **Table 1**. The study area was 32234.29 hectares. **Figure 4** also shows the distribution of land uses in the study area. As the figure shows, most of the barren land is located to the south and north of the city. Agricultural lands are scattered around the city, especially in the eastern, western, and northern parts of the city. An important

Legend	Hectares	Percent
Barren Land(bare land and light artificial forest)	11366.73	35.26
Green Space(mass and light vegetation and agricultural lands)	7999.18	24.82
Built-up(residential lands)	5750.16	17.84
Barren land(uncultivated land, shrub and grass)	7118.22	22.08
Total	32234.29	100.00

Source: Research Findings.

Table 1.
Classification of land uses in study area of Sarakhs in 2020.

point in the land use classification of 2020 is the lack of proper separation of colors by the IsoCluster classification model, which could not separate the land uses well. In particular, the western and eastern parts of the city, which are barren, are classified as residential.

4.2 Trend of spatial expansion of the city

Managing and guiding the future growth of the city require studying the physical expansion of the city in the past and present. Therefore, using Landsat 7 and 8 satellite images in 2003 and 2020, the city limits and the process of its physical expansion were determined through the Digitize command in TerrSet software (**Figure 6**). As can be seen from the figure, the built-up area of Sarakhs for 2003 and 2020 was 439 and 684 hectares, respectively (55.80% growth). In addition, the spatial development of the city has been in different directions. The important point is that the urban growth of the city, in the Master Plan, was projected on the barren lands in the north and south of the city in 2016. The expansion of the city has to some extent been in line with the proposal of the Master Plan until 2020, but most of the spatial expansion of the city has been on agricultural lands and around the roads to the west and east of the city.

4.3 Urban growth in the Master Plan

As mentioned in the earlier sections, cities are gradually growing. To guide the city's spatial expansion, the city administration determines the Master Plan which delineates the future development direction of the city according to the population growth trend in a new coming 15-year period. The comprehensive plan tries to expand the spatial future of the city low-value of agricultural production and barren land. In the Sarakhs Master Plan 2016–2030, according to the calculation of 2%

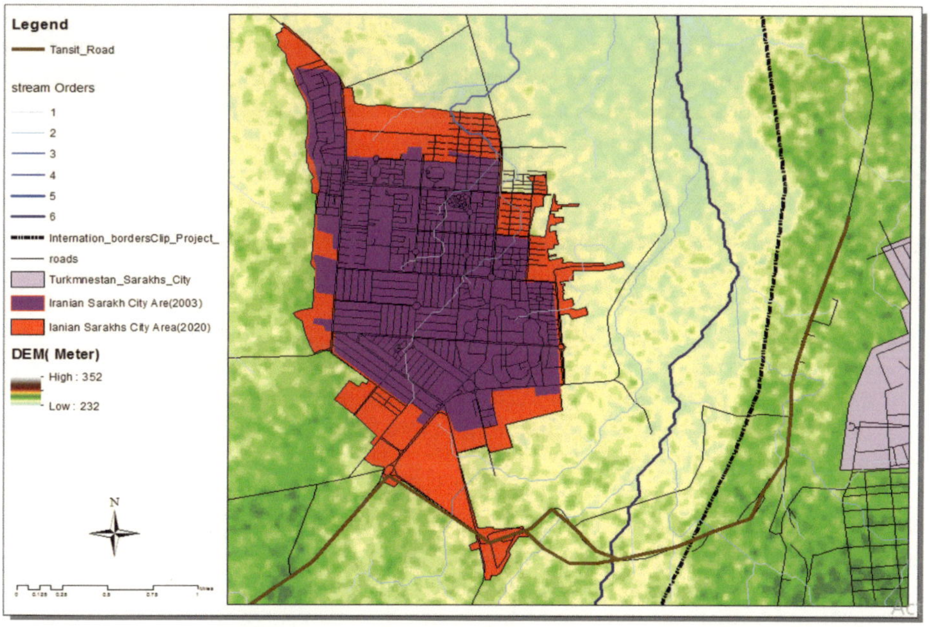

Figure 6.
The trend of spatial expansion of Sarakhs city during the period 2003–2020.

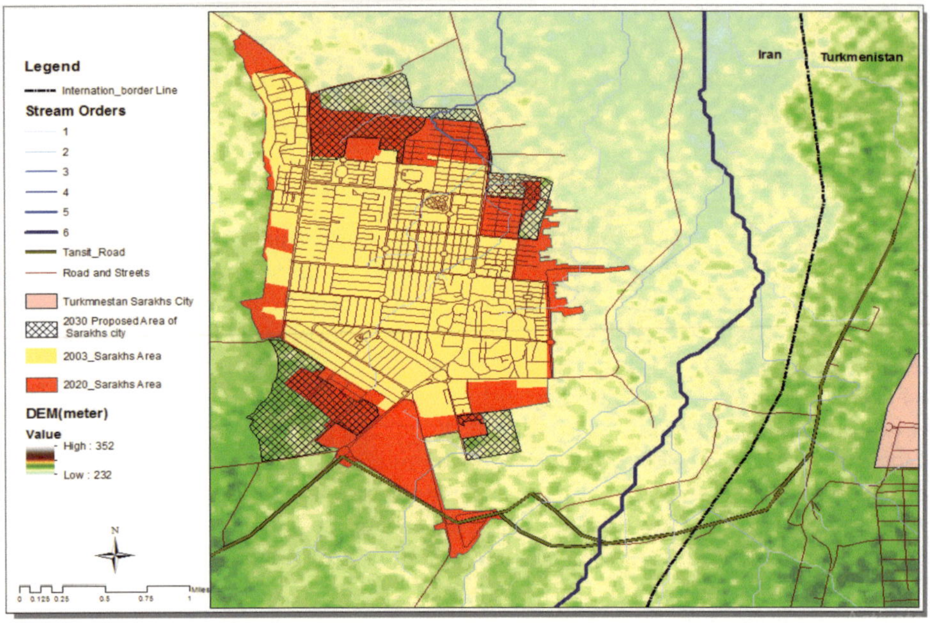

Figure 7.
Spatial development of Sarakhs's Master Plan 2016–2030.

annual population growth, 322 hectares of required land use have been proposed on vacant and barren lands in and around the city. The lattice area in **Figure 7** shows the proposed land use of the Master Plan until 2030 [19].

4.4 Result of designing a spatial decision model for projecting of urban growth

The purpose of this study has two objectives for locating the future residential and industrial development of the city with a MOLA model. A total of 13 variables affects the site selection of residential and industrial land uses. These variables include three categories: (1) constraint variable, (2) common variables, and (3) special variables (**Figure 8**). In general, nine variables were used for selecting an industrial site and eight variables for residential location. Among these, one variable is as a constraint (agricultural land use) and five are common variables between two objects (residential and industrial land uses). A number of specific variables for each object were identified separately (four land uses for industrial and three for a residential objects). These variables play a decisive role in site selection. This situation is shown in **Figure 8**. Therefore, according to the objectives of preparing comprehensive urban plans in Iran in the next 15 years, the SDM was designed in the form of **Figure 8**. In this model, research variables, Fuzzy membership functions, and results are identified along with an MCE and MOLA models.

Given the number of populations that will be added to the city's population by 2030 (20,000 people) and the land required for this population (322 hectares of residential and 500 hectares for industrial activities), the main issue was the location of this land uses. Where should these areas be located? To find the best location for residential and industrial land uses of the city in the SDM according to the research objectives, it should be in line with sustainable environmental development. Initially, several assumptions were made. These hypotheses were determined according to

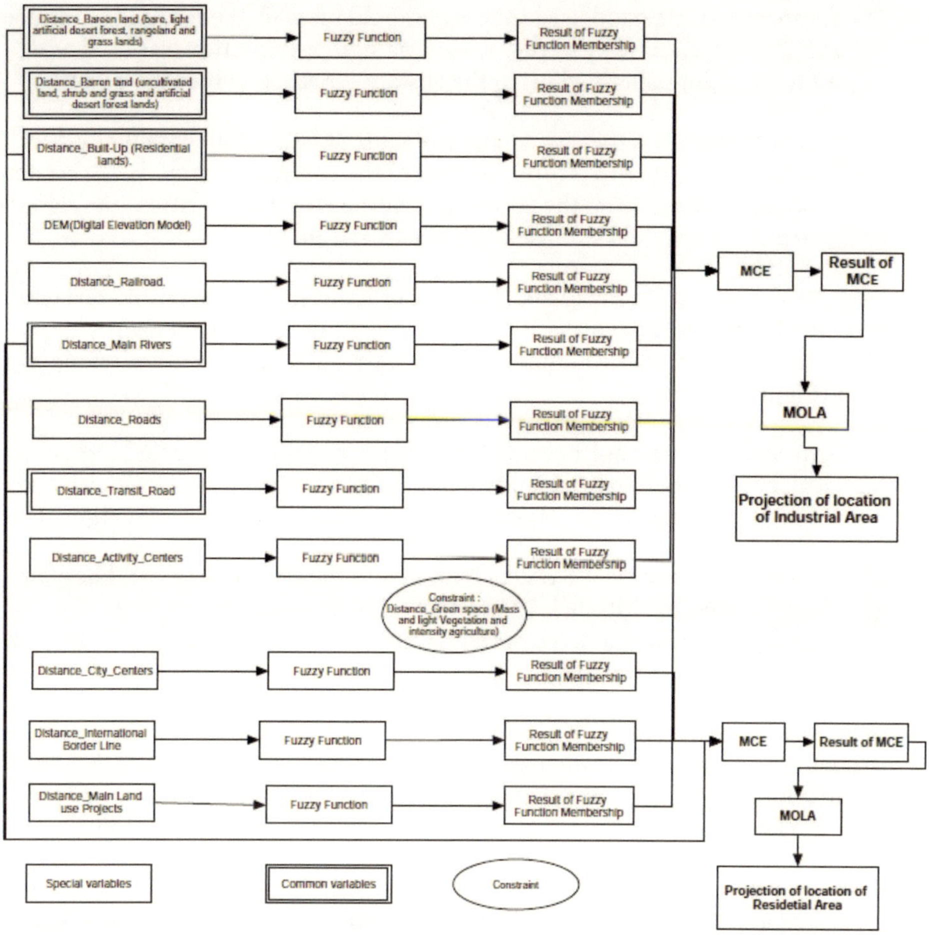

Figure 8.
Structured framework of spatial decision model.

the research objectives, a number of driving factors, the trend of physical expansion of the city from 2003 to 2020, analyzing the land use map in 2020, and studying the results of locating the city development in the Master Plan. These indicators are the main background for the formation of hypotheses and research models. These hypotheses are as follows:

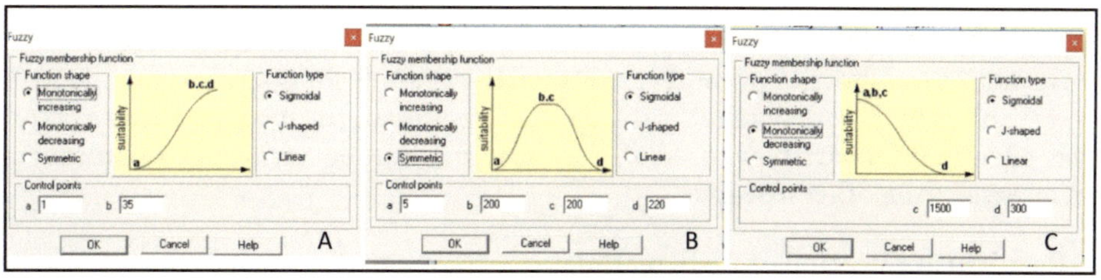

Figure 9.
Sigmoid fuzzy function scheme for increasing, decreasing and symmetry conditions: A = monotonically increasing sigmoidal, B = symmetric sigmoidal, C = monotonically decreasing sigmoidal.

1. The future residential land use of the city should be available next to the residential use. Therefore, to fuzzy it, the symmetric sigmoid equation was used with respect to the values obtained using the Distance method (**Figures 8** and **9A**).

2. With the distance from the city center, the value of land should gradually decrease, until urban growth is directed toward the compact city model. According to the values obtained from the application of the Distance equation, the sigmoid symmetric fuzzy method was used (**Figures 8** and **9B3**).

3. With the distance from the roads, the value of lands for industrial and residential uses should gradually decrease. According to the values obtained from the application of the Distance equation, the Symmetric Sigmoid fuzzy technique was used (**Figures 8** and **9A**).

4. With the distance from agricultural lands, the value of lands should increase. In fact, residential and industrial lands should not be located on agricultural land. Agricultural land entered the equation as protection and constraint (**Figure 8**).

5. Considering that the city of Sarakhs is located in the low slope of Sarakhs plain and the difference in altitude is 232 and 380 m above sea level, respectively. According to the values obtained from the application of the Distance equation, the sigmoid symmetric fuzzy method has been used (**Figures 8** and **9A**).

6. With the distance from barren lands, the value of lands should increase. In fact, residential and industrial land uses should be located on barren lands. According to the values obtained from the application of the Distance equation, the Monotonically increasing Sigmoid fuzzy technique was used (**Figures 8** and **9B**).

7. With the distance from the international transit road, the value of lands for industrial and residential uses will gradually increase. According to the values obtained from the application of the Distance equation, the Symmetric Sigmoid fuzzy technique was used (**Figures 8** and **9A**).

8. Due to the possibility of flooding of major rivers and the destruction of residential and industrial areas and the preservation of agricultural lands around rivers, these land uses should be away from the river. Therefore, according to the values obtained from the application of the Distance equation, the Symmetric Sigmoid fuzzy method has been used (**Figures 8** and **9A**).

Therefore, due to numerous fuzzy membership functions on the one hand and the number of variables and their importance in the site selection (residential and industrial land), on the other hand, three fuzzy membership functions were used. The results of the above hypotheses are shown in **Figure 9**. Points a, b, c, and d are control points [26]. Perhaps the most important feature of the model is the design of fuzzy equations for variables based on the above assumptions, which distinguishes this research from other research.

4.5 Result of application of MCE technique

In MCE, different factors are combined in a suitable plan or goal. First, the weight of each variable (13 variables except agricultural land variable) was calculated using the AHP option, based on the Saati table (weights 1–9). The weight of each variable for the purposes of residential and industrial sites was determined in **Tables 2** and **3**. As shown in **Table 2** for residential land use, the three factors of distance from agricultural land (0.5034), distance from residential lands (0.2688), and distance from roads (0.1505) have more weight than other variables. The stability coefficient obtained from the calculation of real judgments of the random matrix index is 0.07, which is reliable [27]. Furthermore, in **Table 3**, distance from major centers of activity (0.2898), distance from transit road (0.1695), and distance from railway (0.1501) have more weight than other variables of industrial land use. The calculation of real judgments for the random matrix index is 0.08, which is reliable.

In general, in MCE, an attempt is made to combine a set of factors to achieve a single composite basis for decision-making according to a specific goal, which is done here.

Factor (variable)	Factor (variable) weight
Distance_Built-Up (Residential lands)	0.1526
Distance_Main Rivers	0.0409
Distance_International Line Border	0.0770
Distance_Barren land (bare, light artificial desert forest, rangeland, and grass lands)	0.1465
Distance_Barren land (uncultivated land, shrub, and grass and artificial desert forest lands)	0.0343
Distance_Main land use projects	0.2344
Distance_Transit Road	0.0246
Distance_City Center	0.2898
Consistency ratio = 0.07, Consistency is acceptable.	

Table 2.
The eigenvector of residential weights.

Factor (variable)	Factor (variable) weight
Distance_Built-Up (Residential lands)	0.0981
Distance_Main Rivers	0.0465
Distance_Barren land (bare, light artificial desert forest, rangeland, and grass lands)	0.0908
DEM(Digital Elevation Model)	0.0458
Distance_Barren land (uncultivated land, shrub and grass, and artificial desert forest lands)	0.0782
Distance_Transit_Road	0.1659
Distance Railroad	0.1501
Distance Roads Sarakhs	0.1167
Distance Activity Centers	0.2079
Consistency ratio = 0.08, Consistency is acceptable.	

Table 3.
The eigenvector of industrial weights.

4.6 Simulation of location of future residential and industrial land uses by MOLA model

The main purpose of this research was to locate residential and industrial land uses. So to locate the future development of residential (332 hectares) and industrial land uses (500 hectares) with SDM and MOLA problems, the two above-mentioned targets must first be routinely created from the MCE (**Figure 8**). As the name implies, this option allows you to select multiple targets at the same time, such as locating residential, industrial, and so on. The MOLA operator in the spatial decision model is a way to solve the land allocation problem. Based on the information of several suitable unit goals or maps, MOLA determines the best solution according to the specified limitations. According to the required amount of residential (322 hectares) and industrial (500 hectares) land, and a map raster format marked with a cell with a resolution of 10 m, about 32,200 cells for residential use and 50,000 cells for industrial land uses entered the equation. As a result, the residential and industrial land uses of Sarakhs in 2030 were identified in **Figure 10**. Residential land use was located discretely and continuously on barren lands around the city of Sarakhs. Industrial land use has been determined in the southwest with the distance from the city on barren lands and next to the transit road, railways, and major centers of economic activities such as the airport, railway terminal, and SEZ. These results indicate the model's ability to locate the proposed land uses.

4.7 Validation of simulation results of MOLA model with Sarakhs Master Plan

As mentioned earlier, the Master Plan plans are prepared using the traditional field survey approach and its combination with natural maps. More recently, these plans have been prepared by overlaying different layers and field observations using

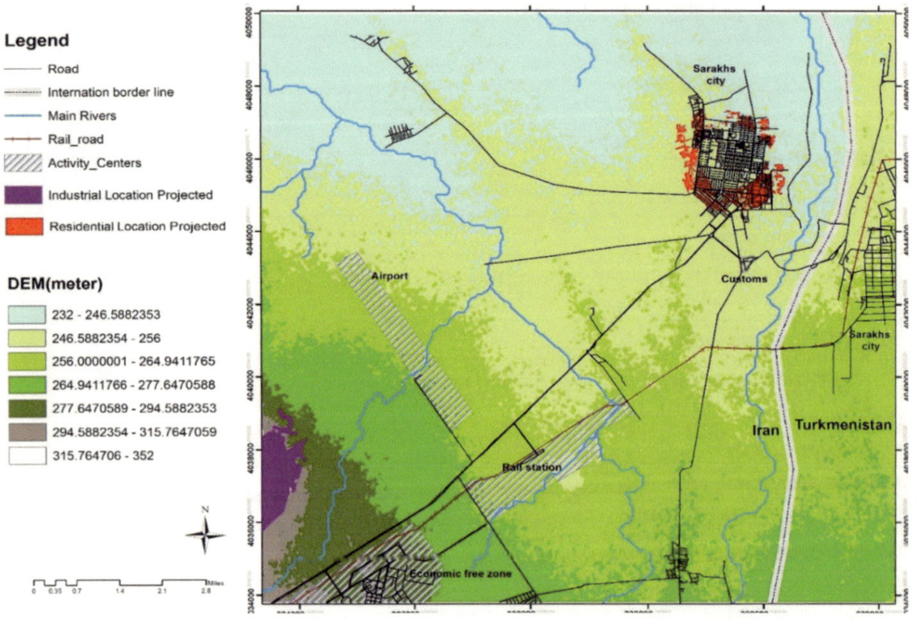

Figure 10.
Simulation of the location of future residential and industrial land uses of Sarakhs city based on MOLA model.

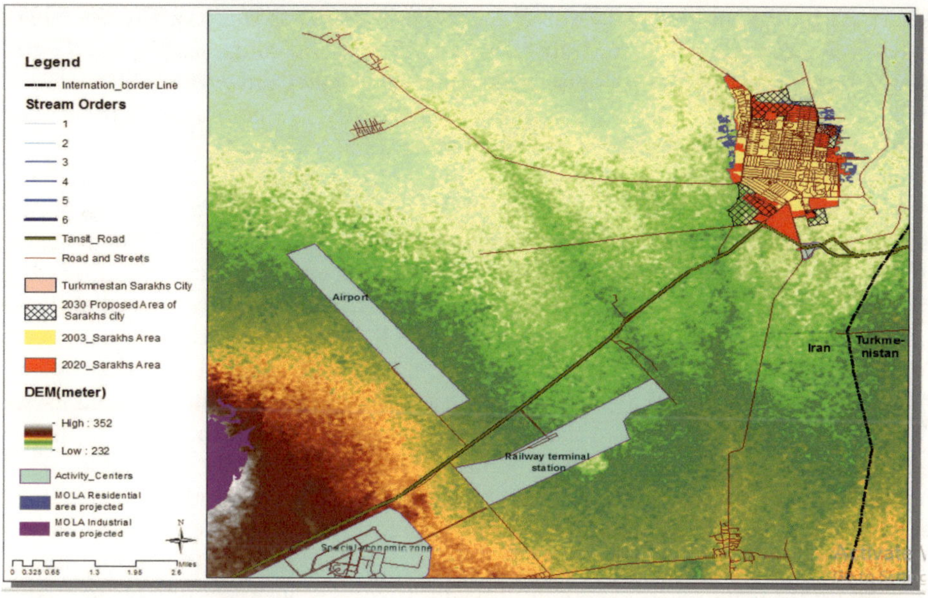

Figure 11.
Validation of the proposed development side of the Master Plan and MOLA model of Sarakhs city.

GIS tools. An example of such a plan is the comprehensive plan of the city of Sarakhs, which is projected as a discrete black checkered grid in the south and north of the city on barren lands. In addition, a special economic zone has been designed on the western side of the city with a 15 km distance (**Figure 11**). The results of using the MOLA model according to 13 variables, research hypotheses, and Fuzzy and AHP techniques show the compliance of residential land use with the proposed results of the city Master Plan on barren lands (**Figure 11**). Meanwhile, industrial land use was proposed in the southwest of the city on barren lands and in the north of the SEZ, next to the transit road, railway terminal, and airport. This relative overlap of the residential land use of the MOLA model and the comprehensive plan on the one hand and the proximity of the industrial land use with the major centers of economic and industrial activities, on the other hand, show the ability of the model to find different objects with high speed, reasonable accuracy, and low cost. This is a feature of the application of spatial allocation models in optimizing the goal and minimizing the cost and can support the urban management decision-making system. However, until now, this procedure has not been used in site selection and urban growth simulation. Internet reviews also confirm this. Although the simulation of urban growth has been done with cellular automation and neural network models, single-purpose and multipurpose land allocations are one of the things that can be used in urban planning to replace the traditional process of preparing Master Plans (**Figure 11**). The proposed development side of the comprehensive plan and MOLA model of Sarakhs city is validated.

5. Discussion

The change in the use of agricultural land, especially around cities (1.8–2.5% of arable land) as a result of the rapid growth of urbanization in Asia (1.7%) and Africa (2.3%) [28], makes it necessary to control urban growth with new tools.

Urban Master Plans have been a tool to control urban growth traditionally since 1947 in developed countries [29], and since 1967 in Third World countries [29, 30]. Until now, the method of preparing these plans has been manual and with traditional tools, which was time consuming, imprecise, and costly. The combination of GIS and spatial decision-making models can help to solve these problems.

In this research, the urban growth of Sarakhs city with the MOLA model in the form of two goals of residential and industrial land use from 2020 to 2030 has been estimated, and these results are compared with the proposal of the traditional Sarakhs Master Plan. The urban growth of the city is simulated on the barren lands around the city using remote sensing data and TerrSet and ArcGIS software. Spatial decision-making model, Fuzzy-AHP technique, MCE, and MOLA techniques were used for the vision of the city by 2030. The MOLA model makes this possible, to select one or more different objects at the same time, such as residential and industrial land uses. The results of the study showed that the built-up area of Sarakhs increased from 439 to 684 hectares from 2003 to 2020. In addition, the results of using 13 variables affecting the location of residential and industrial land uses with the combined fuzzy-HP technique and the MCEA model showed that the factors influencing the location of land uses have different weights. For residential land use location simulation, the three factors of distance from agricultural land (0.5034), distance from residential land (0.2688), and distance from roads (0.1505) have more weight than other variables. The stability coefficient obtained from the calculation of real judgments for the stochastic matrix index was 0.07, which was reliable [27]. Also, for industrial sites, the factors of distance from major centers of activity (0.2898), distance from transit road (0.1695), and distance from the railway (0.1501) have more weight than other variables. The stability coefficient obtained from the calculation of real judgments for the stochastic matrix index was equal to 0.08, which was reliable. Finally, using the MOLA model, considering the area of residential and industrial land use for 2030, which is equal to 322 and 500 hectares, respectively. Residential land uses were sporadically located along barren lands around the city to the north, west, east, and south of the city (**Figure 10**). Meanwhile, the proposed development of industrial land on barren lands was located at a distance from agricultural lands and adjacent to major roads, centers of activity, and transit roads in the south-west of Sarakhs city. These simulations are relatively consistent with the proposed Master Plan of the city. The use of this method to locate the development side of cities has not been observed in online surveys. But Bahadur Thapaa and Murayamab [9] proposed urban growth until 2050 under three scenarios, using artificial neural network for Nepal Kathmandu Valley: To some extent, the results of urban growth simulation of Sarakhs are compatible with the environmental protection scenario of Nepal Kathmandu Valley. The only case identified on the Internet is the application of the MOLA model of the zoning of Iran's Qomishloo Wildlife Sanctuary, allocating suitable land for four purposes of protection, improvement, tourism, and heritage history [10]. The most important difference between this research and other research was summarized in the fact that they first find several options and then prioritize between them, such as prioritizing the selection of municipal landfills with the AHP model [31], combining GIS and allocating space to give optimal health services and locating health centers [23, 32], and prioritizing several sites to select the best place for Solar energy farms [11]. In these examples, several predefined sites are first prioritized as a result of using the model. But in MOLA model, one or more sites are selected from the infinite number of options in the optimal mode. These options are not known in advance. Therefore, the MOLA model is the optimization of the goals according to the status of the factors affecting it. Speed of operation and more accuracy and less cost are the features of using the MOLA model for location-allocation problems for the Third World countries such as Iran with rapid urbanization, especially small-scale cities such as Sarakhs. Due to the weakness of the scientific literature on the use of the MOLA model in allocating space in the preparation of Master Plans, the published scientific experience can no longer be found in the TerrSet software directory. Internet searches on reputable scientific databases also confirm this shortcoming. Further studies on the application of the model in different cities and regions and the selection of effective variables, especially social, economic, and environmental variables, are needed for better result.

6. Conclusions

The presence of more than 50% of the world's population in cities in 2018 and the forecast of its share up to 68% by 2050, raising the need to guide and manage urban growth, especially in Third World countries in the form of preparing Master Plans. These plans, despite being abandoned in developed countries, are major tools for guiding and managing urban growth in Third World cities [33]. Numerous reasons have been cited for the failure of these plans in practice, the long process of traditional methodological preparation of plans, especially site selection of the cities has been one of their major problems. In this study, we tried to simulate the urban growth of Sarakhs as a small border town with a population of fewer than 100,000 people, according to the two purposes of residential and industrial land use with the MOLA model in TerrSet software, and Landsat 7 and 8 satellite images and Sentinel 2A by 2030. The results of applying the MOLA model in the site selection of Sarakhs city with both residential and industrial purposes showed that the model has the ability to simulate such urban growth in such cities. And this simulation is in relative compliance with the prediction results of the traditional city Master Plan. Due to its high speed of operation, high accuracy, time, and cost savings, this model can help guide urban growth to improve the quality of comprehensive plans, which are the dominant model of development in Third World countries. In order to improve the quality of the model, other social, economic, and environmental aspects need to be studied.

Data availability statement

Some or all data, models, or code that support the findings of this study are available from the corresponding author upon reasonable request.

Author details

Mohammad Rahim Rahnama
Faculty of Letters and Humanities, Urban Planning and Geography, Ferdowsi University of Mashhad, Mashhad, Iran

*Address all correspondence to: rahnama@um.ac.ir

References

[1] Guneralp B, Seto K. Futures of global urban expansion: Uncertainties and implications for biodiversity conservation. Environmental Research Letters. 2013;**8**:1-11

[2] d'Amour C, Reitsmac F, Baiocchid G, Barthele S, Güneralpg B, Erbh K-H, et al. Future urban land expansion and implications for global croplands. PNAS. 2017;**14**(30):8939-8944. DOI: 10.1073/pnas.1606036114

[3] Xu C, Liu M, Hong C, Chi T. Temporal variation of characteristic scales in urban landscapes: An insight into the evolving internal structures of China's two largest cities. Landscape Ecology. 2012;**27**:1063-1074. DOI: 10.1007/s10980-012-9764-x

[4] Svoray T, Pua B, Bannet T. Urban land-use allocation in a Mediterranean ecotone: Habitat Heterogeneity Model incorporated in a GIS using a multi-criteria mechanism. Landscape and Urban Planning. 2005;**72**:337-351. DOI: 10.1016/j.landurbplan.2004.05.001

[5] Planning. 04 April 2020. Retrieved from: https://www.a2gov.org/departments/planning/Pages/City-Master-

[6] Sharifia A, Chibab Y, Okamotoc K, Yokoyamac S. Can master planning control and regulate urban growth in Vientiane, Laos? Landscape and Urban Planning. 2014;**131**:1-13. DOI: 10.1016/j.landurbplan.2014.07.014

[7] Nallathiga R. From Master Plan to Vision Plan: The changing role of plans and plan making in city development (with reference to Mumbai). Theoretical and Empirical Researches in Urban Management. 2009;**4**(13):141-157. Retrieved from: https://www.researchgate.net/publication/46567821

[8] Carter JG. Urban climate change adaptation: Exploring the implications of future land cover scenarios. Cities. 2018;**2018**(77):73-80

[9] Bahadur Thapaa R, Murayamab Y. Scenario based urban growth allocation in Kathmandu Valley, Nepal. Landscape and Urban Planning. 2012;**105**:140-148

[10] Hajehforooshniaa S, Soffianian A, Mahinyc A, Fakheranb S. Multi objective land allocation (MOLA) for zoning Ghamishloo Wildlife Sanctuary in Iran. Journal for Nature Conservation. 2011;**19**:254-262. DOI: 10.1016/j.jnc.2011.03.001

[11] Tavana M, Santos Arteaga F, Mohammadi S, Alimohammadi M. A fuzzy multi-criteria spatial decision support system for solar farm location planning. Energy Strategy Reviews. 2017;**18**:93-105. DOI: 10.1016/j.esr.2017.09.003

[12] Commonwealth of Independent States. 2020. Retrieved from: https://en.wikipedia.org/wiki/Commonwealth_of_Independent_States. [Accessed: 23 May 2020]

[13] Statistical Center of Iran. 10 May 2020. Retrieved from: https://www.amar.org.ir/Portals/0/1_result 951221.pdf

[14] Sarakhs Municipality Report. Strategic and Operational Plan of Sarakhs City. Sarakhs: Sarakhs Municipality; 2016

[15] Sarakhs. 23 May 2020. Retrieved from: https://fa.wikipedia.org/wiki/

[16] Williams T. The Silk Roads: An ICOMOS Thematic Study. United Nation: International Council of Monuments and Sites; 2014

[17] University Jihad of Mashhad. Planning Studies of Khorasan Razavi Province; 2015

[18] History Page. 03 April 2020. Retrieved from: http://www.khangiran.com/Pages/History.aspx

[19] Sarakhs Strategic-Operational Plan. Sarakhs: Sarakhs Manicipality; 2019

[20] Explorer E. EarthExplorer—Home. 2020. Retrieved from: https://earthexplorer.usgs.gov/ [13 July 2020]

[21] Europe's Eyes on Earth. 2020. Retrieved from: https://www.copernicus.eu/en. [Accessed: 23 June 2020]

[22] Extract.bbbike. 2020. Retrieved from: https://extract.bbbike.org/ [Accessed: 12 March 2020]

[23] Bernard Keenana P, Jankowsk P. Spatial decision support systems: Three decades on. Decision Support Systems. 2019;**116**:64-76. DOI: 10.1016/j.dss.2018.10.010

[24] Schmidt K, Aumann I, Hollander I, Damm K, J-Matthias G. Applying the analytic hierarchy process in healthcare research: A systematic literature review and evaluation of reporting. BMC Medical Informatics and Decision Making. 2015;**15**(112):1-27. DOI: 10.1186/s12911-015-0234-7

[25] Eastman J. TeerSet, Geospatial Monitoring and Modeling System. Clark Labs, Clark University; 2020. Retrieved from: https://clarklabs.org/ [Accessed: 04 April 2020]

[26] Bicca Oliveira D, Rodrigues J, Ferreira da Silva L, Sanches Oliveira P. Multi-criteria analysis in the strategic environmental assessment of the sugar and alcohol sector. Acta Scientiarum. 2012;**34**(3):303-311. DOI: 10.4025/actascitechnol.v34i3.11525

[27] Alonso J, Lamata M. Consistency in the analytic hierarchy process: A new approach. International Journal of Uncertainty, Fuzziness and Knowledge-Based Systems. 2006;**14**(4):445-459. Retrieved from: https://worldscientific.com/

[28] World Urban Population. 10 May 2022. Retrieved from: https://statisticstimes.com/

[29] Hameed R, Nadeem O. Challenges of implementing urban Master Plans: The Lahore experience. World Academy of Science, Engineering and Technology. 2006;**24**:101-108. Retrieved from: http://citeseerx.ist.psu.edu/viewdoc/download?doi=10.1.1.193.204&rep=rep1&type=pdf

[30] Madanipour A. Urban planning and development in Tehran. Cities. 2006;**32**(6):433-438. DOI: 10.1016/j.cities.2006.08.002

[31] Changa N-B, Parvathinathanb G, Breed J. Combining GIS with fuzzy multicriteria decision-making for landfill siting in a fast-growing urban region. Journal of Environmental Management. 2008;**87**:139-153. DOI: 10.1016/j.jenvman.2007.01.011

[32] Khadivi M, Fatemi Ghomi S. Solid waste facilities location using of analytical network process and data envelopment analysis approaches. Waste Management. 2012;**32**(6):1258-1265. DOI: 10.1016/j.wasman.2012.02.002

[33] Yun C, Cantada H. Challenges to Implementing Urban Master Plans—What Are We Missing? 25 February 2019. Retrieved from: https://blogs.worldbank.org/sustainablecities/challenges-implementing-urban-master-plans-what-are-we-missing [26 August 2020]

Section 2

Urban Land Use Planning

Chapter 3

Implementation and Management of Urban Land Use Plans in Ghana

Issaka Kanton Osumanu

Abstract

The growth and expansion of urban areas come with benefits and challenges due to their enigmatic nature. As a result, towns and cities need land-use plans to direct and promote their growth in an organized manner to enable a realization of their benefits. Land use plans do not come to any meaningful thing if they are not implemented and managed effectively. This chapter assesses the implementation and management of land use plans in growing cities in Ghana. The chapter is based on a systematic review of existing literature and observations. The findings establish that urban land use planning in Ghana has adopted the three-tier land-use planning model which considers spatial planning at various levels and the types of plans that will be prepared to address the needs of all stakeholders. Urban land-use plan implementation and management in the country are thwarted by slow, cumbersome, and unending land delivery processes, weak participatory approach to land use planning, obsolete land-use policies and methods, and insufficient human and financial resources. Legislations and stakeholder participation are needed in plan preparation, implementation, and management.

Keywords: growing cities, benefits, challenges, techniques, guided growth

1. Introduction

An increase in urban populations from natural growth, net rural–urban migration, and the expansion of urban economies induce the physical expansion of cities. In 1950, 30% of the world's population was urban. In 2014, 54% of the global population lived in urban areas and, by 2050, 66% of the population is estimated to be urban [1]. In Africa, the rate of urbanization increased from 15% in 1960 to 40% in 2010 and is estimated to reach 60% in 2050. It is expected that urban populations in Africa will triple in the next 50 years [2]. According to Oloyede [3], countries like Kenya, Nigeria, and Ghana double their populations every 17 years, with key cities in these countries growing faster by characteristic yearly increases of 10%.

Ghana, like many African countries, is fast urbanizing as a result of rapid urban growth fuelled by a high birth rate, rural–urban migration, and intensified economic liberalization and globalization [4, 5]. In 2020, Ghana was urbanizing at a rate of 3.26% annually and 57.35% of the country's total population was found in towns and cities [6]. The growth of urban the population necessitates additional space (land) for residential and other urban infrastructural development. According to Osumanu et al. [5], as urban centers grow in size, there is always a high demand for land for different uses and purposes. In Ghana, the growth of cities and towns comes with sporadic physical development in the context of municipal authorities' inability to minimize the negative externalities associated with rapid expansion while increasing the benefits of urbanization [7, 8]. This threatens urban development and sustainable urbanization [2].

Unmanaged growth of cities and towns in Ghana has resulted in problems including the over-stretching of infrastructural facilities and services, scanty shelter, deteriorating sanitary conditions, chaotic physical developments, and shoddy housing construction [9]. Additionally, it has huge challenges and risks of social tension, insecurity, congestion, and pollution [10]. For a well-organized and orderly urban growth, there is the need for land use plans to direct the expansion in an efficient and sustained manner. Land use plans provide tools and techniques which are used to guide and manage an orderly growth of cities and towns in a deliberate way. As a result, municipal authorities have to prepare land use plans to promote orderly growth and quality environments. Furthermore, completed land use plans come to nothing if they are not properly implemented to conform to their provisions on the ground. According to Feitelson et al. [11], the object of a plan is that its proposals should be put into practice.

The growing problem of violating provisions and proposals in land use plans in urban areas has been a matter of concern in many developing countries, including Ghana. Most of the visible problems challenging urban dwellers as a result of violating the provisions in urban land-use plans include [7, 12–14]:

- Rising vulnerability of urban populations to disasters, resulting from the construction of residential units in areas disposed to floods and other environmental hazards.

- Insufficient shelter, and inadequately maintained and worsening urban physical infrastructure, particularly water supply, sanitation, and energy.

This phenomenon creates several disorders in urban governance and environmental management [14]. City authorities attempt to mitigate these challenges necessitate the preparation of land use plans to guide development in urban areas. As land-use plans are being implemented over time, coupled with the growing nature of cities, there is the need to understand the processes of implementation and management of the plans to be able to take advantage of the opportunities for effective development control mechanisms for sustainable city growth [2]. This chapter assesses the implementation and management of land use plans in growing cities in Ghana. This will allow a connection to be made between plan preparation, implementation, and management. Again, it will aid in clarifying misconceptions and misinformation about land use plans' implementation and management and serve as a basis for policies and program formulation to ensure orderly physical growth and sustainable urban development.

This introductory section is followed by a description of the methodology employed by the study. The third section discusses urban land use planning in Ghana and section four assesses the implementation of urban land use planning by focusing on the factors affecting plan implantation and management. This is followed by a presentation of a case study of urban land use implementation and management in Tamale Metropolitan Area (TMA). Section six concludes the chapter with some policy implications.

2. Methodology

The chapter is based on a review of existing literature and observations. It adopted the Preferred Reporting Items for Systematic Reviews and Meta-Analyses (PRISMA) approach [15] to guide the literature screening and review process. Scopus, Web of Science, JSTOR, and Mendeley literature search were searched for articles and reports relevant to urban growth, planning, and land use plans implementation. Search for phrases and keywords were used together, including urbanization, land use planning plans implementation, and management in Ghana. Google, Google Scholar, and Mendeley were used to search for relevant literature. Websites of ministries and agencies involved in land use planning and implementation were also searched for relevant literature. These were further combined with a manual search of references in all selected articles. The bibliography at the end of each retrieved article was sought after should the article discuss a theme on land use plans implementation and management in Ghana.

The following inclusion criteria were employed: (i) urban growth and expansion; (ii) land use planning; (iii) plans implementation and management; (iv) articles were published in English; and (v) articles published from 2010 to 2022. The exclusion criteria were as follows: (i) review articles, case reports, books, guidelines, dissertations, conference proceedings, a consensus of opinions, or other unrelated topics; (ii) those not referring to the association between urban land use planning and plans implantation and management; and (iii) all other languages.

The search strategy and screening of titles and abstracts were conducted against the inclusion criteria. This was followed by an evaluation of full-text articles against the inclusion criteria and the extraction of key information into a spreadsheet. Baseline features and target parameters were then extracted from the selected articles. For each publication, the author, year of publication, and data on land use plan implementation and management were extracted. Furthermore, the data extracted included information on the chapter's objectives, key results, and recommendations. Priori codes that were generated deductively from previous work on land use plans implementation and management were used to group themes from the data. This was achieved by manually reading through each publication and grouping similar themes and sub-themes. Accuracy was ensured by going back to the sources to verify that all information was correctly interpreted. Vital findings were summarized and any takeaway messages concerning my understanding of urban land-use plans implementation and management and gaps were noted for this study. In addition to the systematic review, personal observation was used to provide a case study of the Tamale Metropolitan Area in northern Ghana. This method enabled me to observe the phenomenon of urban land use plan implementation and management in a most natural setting.

3. Urban land use planning in Ghana

Land use planning is an examination of urban activity systems and a careful estimate of future land use requirements for growth and regeneration, showing how development in urban areas should be carried out to ensure the best conceivable physical environment for functional cities, the most economic use of land, and the appropriate balance in use from a cost-revenue point of view [2, 11, 12]. Essentially, an urban land use plan exemplifies a proposal as to how growth and renewal should proceed in the future, taking into consideration local needs and generally accepted principles of health, safety, convenience, economy, and the overall amenities for urban living. Generally, a primary objective of urban land use planning is to control the development and use of land in the public interest.

Over the years, urban land use planning in Ghana has adopted a three-tier land-use planning model (**Figure 1**). This model considers spatial planning at various levels and the types of plans that will be prepared to address the needs of all stakeholders. It enables a spatial development framework (SDF) to be formulated for the country, a region, a municipality, or a development corridor. The SDF serves as a framework that expresses the socio-economic policies of an area in a spatial form. It, therefore, provides a spatial expression of how the urban area will look like if it implements its socio-economic policies over a while. Such a spatial expression will interact with social and economic policies to disclose new potentials and synergies for development. According to the Ministry of Environment Science and Technology (MEST) [16], the SDF covers 20 years and makes provisions for the kinds of development that should take place, how much of it should happen, and where and how this should occur to take advantage of emerging opportunities.

The second type of plan within the three-tier model is the structure plan. A structure plan is a plan for an urban area that formulates policy and general proposals on social, economic, and spatial aspects of the area [16]. The structure plan is a dimensionally-specific and accurate spatial plan which is used to guide the development or redevelopment of an urban area. It covers 10–15 years and considers the existing situation of a town or city as well as the future needs of the area and then makes a projection for the land required for the area which is expressed in a broader perspective.

Next to the structure plan in the hierarchy of the model in **Figure 1** is the local plan. The local plan is a comprehensive and detailed plan which shows the arrangement or disposition of various land uses. It is a digitized, dimensionally-precise layout plan of an area under development that shows individual plots of land, open lands, amenities, movement and transport systems, power, water, and sanitation [17]. The

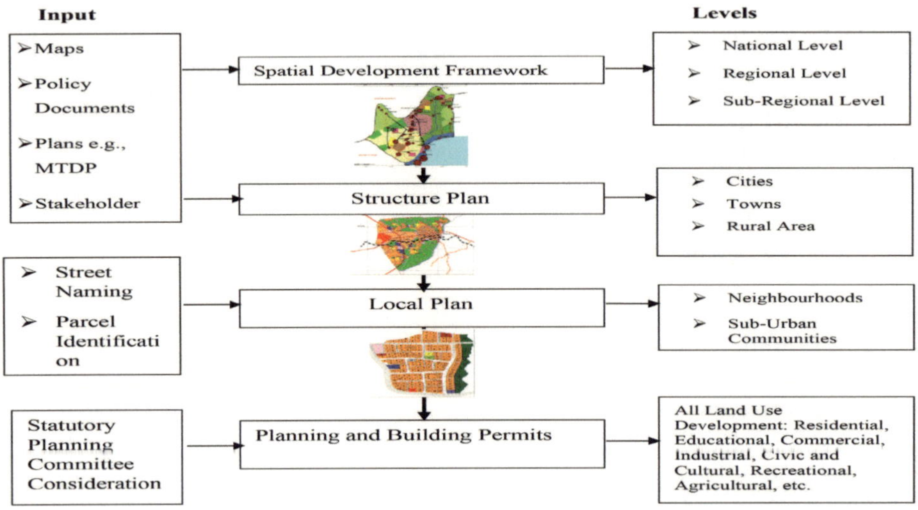

Figure 1.
The three-tier spatial planning model. Source: MEST [16].

local plan is a spatial plan for a neighborhood or sub-community from which a building permit is granted by the planning authority to developers [16]. The implementation of local plan proposals and development going according to the plan benefits the area in terms of street naming and parcel identification.

The three-tier planning model stresses stakeholders' participation at all levels of spatial plan preparation and implementation. This will ensure that communities are aware of the proposals in these plans and feel that they own the plans which will enable them to contribute effectively to the implementation and management of the plans [11, 14].

The Land Use and Spatial Planning Act (Act 925) defines a planning area as the territory of Ghana as defined under the Constitution of the Republic of Ghana including the land mass, air space, sub-terrain territory, marine space, and reclaimed lands [18]. According to the Act, the framework for spatial planning in Ghana comprises:

a. the National and Sub-National Spatial Development Framework, which covers the entire country or a part of it including marine space, where the context requires;

b. a Regional Spatial Development Framework for each of the administrative regions of the country or Joint-Regional Spatial Development Framework for multiple regions where appropriate or Sub Regional Spatial Development Framework covering parts of a region where the context requires; or

c. District Spatial Development Framework for each district, or where appropriate, a Joint or Multi-District Spatial Development Framework.

The overall objective of the National Spatial Development Framework is the judicious use of land and the equitable distribution of national infrastructure and facilities in various human settlements of the country. The Regional Spatial Development Framework, Sub-Regional Spatial Development Framework, and Joint or Multi-Regional Spatial Development Framework have their key objectives as the judicious use of land and supportive spatial strategy for exploiting unique regional prospects for increasing regional and national prosperity. The objective of a local plan shall be the judicious use of land for attaining a sound, natural, and built environment and an improved living standard.

4. Implementation of urban land use plans

Planning involves making choices among the opportunities that appear open for the future and securing their implementation, which depends upon the allocation of essential and available resources [19]. Urban land-use planning offers an excellent technique for the management of a range of significant human activities by designing and regulating how people use land and natural resources. Implementation is crucial in the plan preparation process because it is a specified set of actions designed to put into practice all proposed activities or programs of the plan. Development plans articulate policy issues that are suitable for implementation and, to fulfill this role, plans are prepared with written statements, which state the goals and objectives, appropriate policies and proposals, preferred development strategies, and implementation and monitoring modalities [20]. The written statements are reinforced with maps and diagrams that spatially show topographical details, land boundaries, and the dimensions of development proposals. Implementation is the process of bringing the plan into reality [11] and it does not occur overnight. Moreover, if steps are not taken to integrate the plan into existing and new development activities, the result is that the plan becomes a guide for reference [21].

A functional planning system is dependent on effective development control mechanisms which planning authorities, politicians, and communities of beneficiaries of plans expect that the intended outcomes expressed in a proposed plan will be achieved through the implementation process [19]. This means that if plans are not executed appropriately, the desired outcomes would not be achieved.

Land use plan implementation tools are the techniques that are adopted to ensure that provisions made in land use plans are implemented according to plan. Physical development is guided and controlled by planning and implementation tools that are grounded in the preparation of spatial plans and detailed intentions and uses [20]. In Ghana, the land-use implementation tools employed are development control, legal protection of plans, zoning regulations, land subdivision regulations, building regulations, and urban renewal programs [16].

4.1 Factors that affect the implementation and management of urban land use plans

Successful implementation and management of urban land-use plans depend on many factors including judicious allocation of resources in a coordinated manner. A town or city which is well planned has the following contribution to the overall physical development of the area:

i. It facilitates the effective delivery of infrastructural facilities;

ii. It does not allow non-conformed uses of land in the same place;

iii. It puts land into maximum use; and

iv. It improves the quality of the environment.

The physical development of an urban area is to be guided and directed by planning and implementation instruments [20]. This means the absence of some of the implementation and management factors can affect the smooth operationalization of urban land-use plans which will eventually go against the set objectives of the overall urban development agenda [14].

Implementation is simply the art of executing the provisions in any type of plan and it is very critical in the planning process. One of the implications of the interrelationship of plan preparation and implementation is that many plans are more or less doomed to fail from the start because of the content and mode of the presentation and how they were prepared [11, 19].

Plan implementation and management in growing cities in Ghana are generally influenced by a lot of factors. First, the land delivery process is critical in the implementation and management of urban land-use plans. In Ghana, slow, cumbersome, and unending land delivery processes [22] often delay the acquisition of title to land—a prerequisite for development. Consequently, people ignore the process and enter into the land to develop after obtaining permission from the land owners.

Secondly, there is a weak participatory approach to the plan preparation, implementation, and management process [23]. Participatory urban land use planning is a process by which a town or city works actively to achieve a given socio-economic goal by consciously identifying its problems and taking a course of action to deal with those problems [24]. Participation in the decision process allows plans to meet the needs and aspirations of local people. This, therefore, means that if land-use plans are prepared without involving key stakeholders, their implementation and management can face a lot of challenges. Communities and organizations, a whole town or city, an urban neighborhood, a school, a national park management team, a water management committee, or any other group may all be affected. This, therefore, means that if all the interest groups are not involved in the planning process, an implementation that is like the actual execution will encounter problems.

Out-of-date land use planning policies and obsolete laws and regulations are also important. A major constraint to effective and efficient urban land use plan implementation and management in Ghana is the absence of up-to-date and dynamic laws and regulations to guide and regulate land use and management [21]. Land use and management in urban areas are supposed to be guided by effective policies, laws, and regulations. This is because towns and cities grow with time; the needs of urban dwellers 10 years ago might not be the same today. However, most of these policies, laws, and regulations are very old and outdated which is not serving the purpose of modem cities.

Inadequate manpower is also another factor that affects the implementation and management of urban land-use plans in Ghana. Most growing cities do not have qualified urban and spatial planners to manage the implementation and management of their plans [14]. This, therefore, gives room for unqualified persons to handle very well-prepared land use plans on the ground.

Moreover, there is inadequate financial support for planning activities in Ghana. Financial resources are very crucial for the successful implementation of plans [11], such that without enough financial support, no meaningful plan implementation and management can be achieved. Most municipal authorities in Ghana do not make enough budgetary allocation for the implementation and management of land use plans. For example, a close examination of the national budget for the current and previous financial years reveals that no financial allocations were made directly to urban land use planning. Moreover, local taxes, licensing fees, property rates, etc. are often not adequate for financial planning activities.

Planning and implementation of plans in most Ghanaian cities are still based on outdated methods. Outmoded equipment, rather than geographic information systems (GIS), is still being applied in the implementation and management of most plans which makes it difficult to track effectively the progress of plan implementation [23]. The contribution and benefits of GIS to land use planning are now widely acknowledged so much so that it is being applied in many fields as a tool for spatially-reference analysis and data manipulation [8].

5. Case study: tamale metropolitan area

Considering the aim of the chapter, Tamale Metropolitan Area (TMA) is appropriate. The Metropolis has similar characteristics to the other rapidly growing metropolitan areas in Ghana such as Sekondi-Takoradi and Sunyani. Tamale also has a lot of peri-urban communities which are becoming urbanized due to the expansion of the city. Again, most of these peri-urban communities in the Metropolis have planning schemes to guide their physical expansion and development and also to facilitate the provision of infrastructural facilities.

5.1 Historical and physical development of Tamale

According to the Tamale Physical Development Plan (1970–1985), Tamale was founded around the fourteenth century by the Dagombas. Before the coming of colonial administration to the area, there was a collection of five communities or villages: Dagomba (the largest and also called Chigonaba), Bari, Tishigu, Dohinayili, and Monshie Zongo. The early growth of Tamale was due to economic activities and, later, political and social activities. The development of a market in Tamale and its location on the north–south trade route contributed tremendously to the growth of economic activities. The report stated that in 1905, the Northern Regional capital was moved from Gambaga to Tamale, which made Tamale the focal point for entire northern Ghana and beyond. Administration and social functions were added which intensified its growth as more people moved to the city from different parts of northern Ghana and other parts of the country. Government offices were constructed including key developments such as the hospital, police station, prisons, secondary school, and so on.

Tamale was growing and expanding, but there was no conscious planning until 1954. The growth of the town was therefore organic since planning had not been introduced to the town. The Planning Department was established in 1955 and the first plan was prepared in 1964 [25]. Before the establishment of the Town Planning Department, the Survey Department carried out the preparation of layouts for some parts of the town. The result of the unconscious early planning and rather organic development of Tamale and its surroundings on its growth gave it a radial-concentric structure. The main roads radiated from the center and outward with the core characterized by commercial activities surrounded by indigenous residential properties and other residential areas. This radial spider webs structure of the city was established which is associated with the organic growth and has dictated the urban structure of the Metropolis till today.

According to TCPD [25], between 1961 and 1968, eight planning schemes were prepared for Wards D, I, M, A, Nim Avenue, Kukuo, Choggu, and Choggu Manayili. The planning activities undertaken were piecemeal at the time until 1969, when the then Director of Town and Country Planning directed that all regional and district capitals should have 15-year physical development plans. Thus, the first plan for Tamale—Tamale Physical Development plan, 1970–1985 (see **Figure 2**)—was prepared. In line with the government's development policy to adopt a growth-pole strategy at the time, Tamale was designated as one of the national growth centers or poles in the country and the need for a plan could not be overemphasized. The growth of Tamale has therefore been guided by the 1970–1985 plan, though implemented with modifications over the years. The plan was for a projected population of 374,000 over its 1970 population of 98,818. According to TCPD [25], there was a minor revision in 1999 but there is a need for the plan to be comprehensively revised to meet current development challenges.

5.2 Types of land use plans in the Tamale Metropolis

An urban land use plan is a conception of the spatial arrangement of land uses with a set of proposed actions to make it a reality [20]. Land use plans are therefore

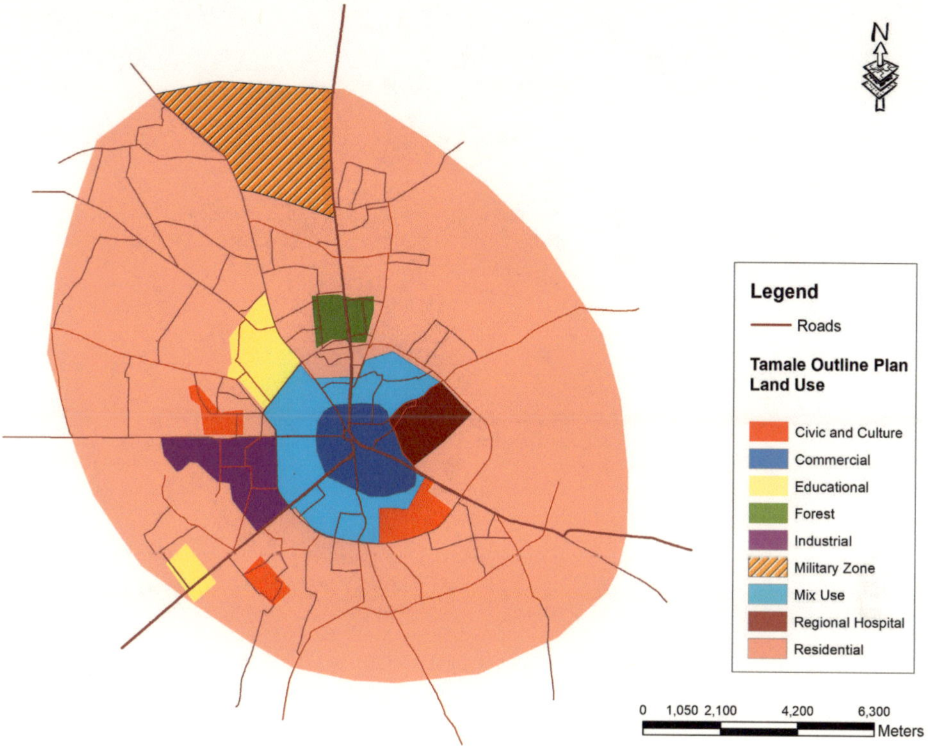

Figure 2.
Tamale physical development plan (1970–1985). Source: TCPD [25].

prepared for different levels of spatial development with a linkage relationship between higher-level plans and lower-level plans. The SDF is mostly for a nation, region, district, or development corridor [16]. The structure plan is prepared to guide the growth of urban areas in a broader land-use perspective while the local plan is meant for a section or neighborhood of a city.

In TMA, the most popular and available land-use plans for implementation are local/sector layouts (**Figure 3**) with less focus on SDF and Structure plans. This is not compliant with the objectives of the three-tier spatial planning model in Ghana [16] that structure plans provide the framework within which all local plans for a city or town should comply. This situation creates a missing link and improper coordination in land-use implementation and management in the Metropolis. It also allows plans to be prepared for only sections of communities without proper needs assessment for the entire Metropolis, a situation which might neglect certain sensitive community needs and also make it impossible for growth poles to be established in the area.

5.3 Implementation and management of land use plans in Tamale Metropolitan Area

Implementation and management are crucial in the plan preparation process because they are specified sets of actions designed to put into practice all proposed activities of a plan. It is at this stage that the intentions of the plan are executed to the realization of set objectives. Effective implementation and management of plans depend on efficient and committed institutional arrangements as well as

Figure 3.
Example of a local plan in TMA. Source: TCPD [25].

the availability of resources [21]. The implementation and management of land use plans in TMA is the responsibility of the land sector agencies such as the Land Use and Spatial Planning Authority (LUSPA), Lands Commission, and the Tamale Metropolitan Assembly (TaMA). Also, land use plan preparation has a lot of components that are handled by separate organizations and for that matter, roles are assigned to institutions in the implementation and management of the plans.

Some basic techniques and strategies are adopted by institutions in TMA to ensure that provisions made in land use plans are implemented according to plan. The basic techniques and strategies are enforcement notice, zoning and planning regulations, demarcation of approved plans, and granting of development permits.

Implementation and management of land use plans in TMA are hindered by many factors. The land delivery system in the Metropolis is slow, cumbersome, and unending which delays the acquisition of title to land—a prerequisite for development. Also, the land ownership system is characterized by land title insecurity, encroachment of public lands, multiple sale of lands, and general land market indiscipline. These challenges in the land ownership system are associated with the inability of land sector agencies to effectively implement and manage land use plans. Again, the Metropolitan LUSPA and TaMA, the main institutions responsible for the implementation and management of land use plans, are faced with inadequate staff and logistics. Other challenges include a weak participatory approach to plan preparation and weak land-use policies and regulations.

LUSPA is a service delivery agency under the Ministry of Environment, Science, Technology, and Innovation (MESTI). It is a decentralized institution that operates at the national and regional levels. At the Metropolitan level, LUSPA provides technical guidance for the physical planning department of TaMA with the main responsibility of preparing human settlement plans and related services to guide and control the physical development of the Metropolis [26]. LUSPA has the responsibility of planning and land use management to ensure and promote the orderly growth and development of human settlements in the Metropolis, which will contribute to quality living environments and sustainable urbanization. The Authority plays a crucial role in the preparation and implementation of land use plans in the Metropolis. It also does a supervisory, monitoring, and coordinating role in spatial planning matters within the Metropolis [26]. As part of its mandate, the Authority prepares land use plans to guide the orderly growth and development of settlements as well as process development applications for approval by the statutory planning committee of TaMA.

Land use plan preparation in TMA is not participatory enough because consultation is limited to only chiefs and their elders with the belief that the views of these people represent that of the communities. Currently, land use plans are prepared based on demand or requests from sub-chiefs through their paramount chiefs. LUSPA meets with the chiefs and elders for them to establish the boundaries of the intended land and any other parcel in the area after a request has been made to the authority to explain the processes involved in the plan preparation. The Survey and Mapping Division of the Lands Commission is contacted for a base map that details the existing structures on the ground after which a plan is prepared. A plan is a draft form that is then presented to the chiefs and elders for their input before the planning committee of TaMA approves the final implementation plan. The plan is then forwarded to the chiefs/land owners by requesting them to engage the services of qualified surveyors, specifically the Survey and Mapping Division, to do demarcations. Mostly, the chiefs tend to use unqualified professionals for the fact that some of them do not know the right surveyors and also with the view that the charges of the official surveyors are high. The current plan preparation procedure does not allow socio-economic data to be collected, and analyzed and needs assessment done before coming out with proposals in the plan. Thus, planning proposals are based on conjunctures or coarse assumptions that people should be given what ought to be and not based on reliable estimates of wants. Also, most of the land use plans in the Metropolis are not covered by official reports, and, for that matter, implementation and management strategies are not spelled out. This, therefore, means that the plans might not be addressing the aspirations of the people which can affect their implementation and management.

6. Conclusion: some policy implications

Towns and cities in Ghana are fast expanding with daunting challenges for orderly physical development. Rapid urbanization and the increasing need for urban infrastructure have escalated the need for effective implementation and management of land use plans. This chapter has assessed the implementation and management of urban land-use plans in growing Ghanaian cities. It has also presented a case study of land use implementation and management in TMA. The lack of effective implementation and management of urban land use plans in the country is a reflection of the slow, cumbersome, and unending land delivery process, weak participatory approach to land use planning, outdated and outmoded land-use policies and methods, and inadequate manpower and financial resources. This suggests that Ghanaian towns and cities are yet to get prepared for efficient implementation and management of land use plans for sustainable urbanization. Technologies for plan preparation, implementation, and management are still based on outmoded methods instead of GIS techniques which makes it difficult to track the progress of plan implementation.

Weak institutional capacity, coupled with poor coordination in land use planning activities, thwart attempts to implement and manage urban land use plans.

Legislations are needed in the preparation of urban land use plans and their implementation and management because they set the direction for developers to follow and the possible punishment for those who contravene regulations. These regulations then put some level of consciousness into people and guide them to do the right thing to ensure that compliance with land use plan provisions is high. Moreover, one of the key elements in the decentralized development planning system is the participation of local communities in planning decisions that affect them. The preparation of urban land-use plans in Ghana must be participatory and consultative. In the process, key stakeholders must be identified and taken through the stages in the plan preparation process. Besides, draft plans must be displayed in public areas with officers around to explain the proposals to people and take inputs from the public to be incorporated into the final plans. This would also allow for a comprehensive report to be prepared for the plans and their implementation and management strategies spelled.

Conflict of interest

The author declares no conflict of interest.

Author details

Issaka Kanton Osumanu
Department of Geography, Simon Diedong Dombo University of Business and Integrated Development Studies, Wa, Ghana

*Address all correspondence to: kosumanu@ubids.edu.gh

References

[1] United Nations. World Urbanization Prospects 2018. New York: United Nations, Department of Economic and Social Affairs; 2019

[2] UN-HABITAT. Sustainable Urban Development in Africa. Nairobi: UN-HABITAT; 2015

[3] Alabi OM. Prioritizing factors of failure in controlling physical development in Nigerian cities. Journal of Sustainable Development in Africa. 2010;**12**(2):215-231

[4] Owusu G, Oteng-Ababio M, Afutu-Kotey RL. Conflicts and governance of landfills in a developing country city Accra. Landscape and Urban Planning. 2012;**104**(1):105-113. DOI: 10.1016/j.landurbplan.2011.10.005

[5] Osumanu IK, Nyaaba AJ, Tuu NG, Owusu-Sekyere E. From patches of villages to a municipality: Time, space, and expansion of Wa, Ghana. Urban Forum. 2018;**30**:57-74. DOI: 10.1007/s12132-018-9341-8

[6] Ghana Statistical Service. Population and Housing Census. Accra: Ghana Statistical Service; 2020

[7] Boamah NA, Gyimah C, Bediako JKN. Challenges to enforcement of development controls in the Wa municipality. Habitat International. 2012;**36**:136-142. DOI: 10.1016/j.habitatint.2011.06.010

[8] Osumanu IK, Akombangre JN. A growing city: Patterns and ramifications of urban change in Wa, Ghana. Spatial Information Research. 2020;**28**(5):523-536. DOI: 10.1007/s41324-020-00313-1

[9] Satterthwaite D. Urbanization in low- and middle-income nations in Africa, Asia and Latin America. In: Desai V, Potter RB, editors. The Companion to Development Studies. 3rd ed. London and New York: Routledge; 2014. pp. 407-417

[10] Yankson PWK, Bertrand M. Introduction: Challenges of urbanization in Ghana. In: Ardayfio-Schandorf E, Yankson PW, Bertrand M, editors. The Mobile City of Accra: Urban Families, Housing and Residential Practices. Dakar: Council for development of Social Science Research in Africa; 2012. pp. 25-46

[11] Feitelson E, Felsenstein D, Razin E, Stern E. Assessing land use plan implementation: Bridging the performance-conformance divide. Land Use Policy. 2017;**61**:251-264. DOI: 10.1016/j.landusepol.2016.11.017

[12] Cobbinah PB, Erdiaw-Kwasie MO. Urbanization in Ghana: Insights and implications for urban governance. In: Benna UG, Garba SB, editors. Population Growth and Rapid Urbanization in the Developing World. Pennsylvania: IGI Global; 2016. pp. 85-107

[13] Acheampong RA, Agyemang FSK, Abdul-Fatawu M. Quantifying the spatio-temporal patterns of settlement growth in a metropolitan region of Ghana. GeoJournal. 2017;**82**(4):823-840. DOI: 10.1007/s10708-016-9719-x

[14] Osumanu IK. Urban environmental management and governance: Towards a conceptual framework. In: Peprah K, Osumanu IK, Aabeyir R, Sumanu JBB, editors. Environment and Natural Resource Management in Ghana. Accra: Woeli Publications; 2022

[15] Moher D, Liberati A, Tetzlaff J, Altman DG. Preferred reporting items

for systematic reviews and meta-analyses: The PRISMA statement. PLoS Medicine. 2009;**6**(7):1-6. DOI: 10.1371/journal.pmed.1000097

[16] Ministry of Environment, Science and Technology (MEST). Manual for the Preparation of Spatial Development Framework, Structure Plan and Local Plan. Accra: MSET; 2011

[17] Enoguanbhor EC, Gollnow F, Walker BB, Nielsen JO, Lakes T. Key challenges for land use planning and its environmental assessments in the Abuja City-region, Nigeria. Land. 2021;**10**:443. DOI: 10.3390/land10050443

[18] Government of Ghana (GoG). Land Use and Spatial Planning Act. Accra: GoG; 2016. p. 2016

[19] Cobbinah PB, Asibey OA, Gyedu-Pensang YA. Urban land use planning in Ghana: Navigating complex coalescence of land ownership and administration. Land Use Policy. 2020;**99**(C):105054. DOI: 10.1016/j.landusepol.2020.105054

[20] Tasantab JC. Beyond the plan: How land use control practices influence flood risk in Sekondi-Takoradi. Jamba. 2019;**11**(1):638. DOI: 10.4102/jamba.v11i1.638

[21] Awuah KGB, Hammond F, Lamond JE. Benefits of urban land use planning in Ghana. Geoforum. 2014;**57**:37-46. DOI: 10.1016/j.geoforum.2013.09.019

[22] Akrofi EO, Whittal J. Compulsory acquisition and urban land delivery in customary areas in Ghana. South African Journal of Geomatics. 2013;**2**(4):280-295

[23] Awuah KGB, Hammond FN. Determinants of low land use planningregulation compliance rate in Ghana. Habitat International. 2014;**41**:17-23. DOI: 10.1016/j.habitatint.2013.06.002

[24] Kleemann J, Inkoom JN, Thiel M, Sharkar S, Lautenbach S, Fust C. Peri-urban land use pattern and its relation to land use planning in Ghana. West Africa. Landscape and Urban Planning. 2017;**165**:280-294. DOI: 10.1016/j.landurbplan.2017.02.004

[25] Town and Country Planning Department. Manual for the Preparation of Spatial Development Framework, Structure Plan and Local Plan. Accra: Ministry of Environment and Science; 2014

[26] Arko-Adjei A. Adapting Land Administration to the Institutional Framework of Customary Tenure: The Case Study of Peri-Urban Ghana. Amsterdam: IOS Press BV; 2016

Chapter 4

Perspective Chapter: Spatio-Temporal Analysis of Urban Expansion

Dejene Tesema Bulti and Anteneh Lemmi Eshete

Abstract

Understanding the effects of urbanization and formulating sustainable planning strategies begins with an analysis of the dynamics of urban growth at various spatial and temporal scales. Several quantitative methods for analyzing urban expansion and the spatial pattern of urbanized areas have been developed and their applications have been widespread. The choice of an appropriate method for a particular situation depends on different factors, making it difficult for users to make an informed decision and increasing the requirement for knowledge about the various approaches. This chapter gives an overview of the prevailing approaches for spatio-temporal analysis of urban expansion. Given the importance of analyzing the spatio-temporal growth of built-up areas for sustainable urbanization, this chapter provides a good insight into the main features of existing methods. Accordingly, it would help researchers and potential users to undertake effective analysis, balancing between their needs and resource requirements.

Keywords: urban dynamics, urban growth, urban expansion, urban planning, sustainability

1. Introduction

Contemporary urbanization is characterized by the rapid growth of urban populations and the rapid spatial growth of urban areas. Unless properly managed, it can result in serious negative environmental and socioeconomic consequences, such as urban heat islands, reductions in green spaces, insufficient infrastructure and services, and inefficient utilization of resources [1–3]. Analyzing the spatio-temporal dynamics of the built-up area of a particular urban landscape is the primary step in understanding the impacts of urbanization [4]. Knowledge about the spatial pattern and intensity of urban land changes is critical for a variety of issues, ranging from human-environmental interactions and the provision of urban environmental services to land-use policy development for landscape and urban planning toward sustainable urbanization [5].

The focus on urban change detection has recently switched from detection to quantification of change, pattern measurement, and pattern and process analysis of urban expansion [1, 6, 7]. To describe spatial patterns effectively, comprehend how they develop over time, compare one component to others, or statistically explain variations in these patterns, quantitative measures that summarize one or more of their attributes are necessary [8, 9]. Several quantitative methods have also been developed and applied to determine measures of spatial patterns and dynamics of urban landscapes.

The choice of methodologies for spatio-temporal analysis of built-up area expansion is influenced by a number of factors, making it difficult for users to make an informed decision and increasing the requirement for information about the various approaches. This chapter gives an overview of the available approaches for spatio-temporal analysis of urban expansion.

2. Methods of urban expansion analysis

2.1 Urban spatial expansion index

The urban spatial expansion index (USEI) is an indicator proposed to analyze the growth of urban areas in terms of spatial increase in urban land-use classes. It quantifies the magnitude of urban expansion per unit of time over the study period using a linear change model (**Figure 1**). USEI for a particular urban area is computed using Eq. (1). When the unit of time is set to a year, it provides the annual change in built-up areas.

$$USEI = \frac{A_{t1} - A_{t0}}{\Delta t} \tag{1}$$

where A_{t0} and A_{t1} denote areas of built-up land at a time $t0$ and $t1$,respectively, and Δt is the length of time from the time $t0$ to $t1$. When Δt is in a unit of the year, then $USEI$ is the annual average expansion of built-up area over the study period.

This approach provides data on the mean annual quantitative increase in built-up area between the starting and ending years of the study period and/or selected time intervals. It gives constant expansion per unit of time during the study period due to its assumption of linear development. Several studies used the urban spatial expansion index to assess the speed of urban growth in the same study area over different times as well as between different countries. For instance, Dutta et al. [10] used this index to estimate yearly built-up change in the peri-urban areas around Delhi from 1977 to

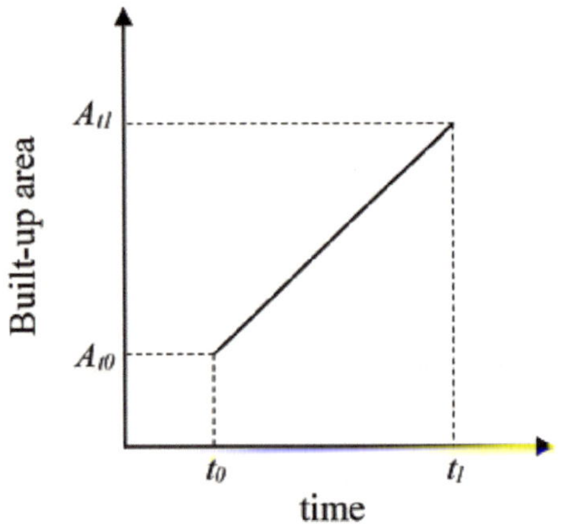

Figure 1.
Linear change model (increments of growth remain constant over time).

2014 by dividing the whole study period into two: 1977–2003 and 2003–2014. The authors then used the results to determine the relationship between built-up change and density. The study conducted by Liu et al. [11] can also be mentioned as a case example of USEI application. In this case, the index was used to gauge the velocity of urban expansion in the Xiaonan District in Hubei Province, China, over a period of every five consecutive years between 1990 and 2020. In relation to the assessment of the infrastructure development contributions to urban expansion, Li et al. [1] used USEI as one of the key indicators of the spatial and temporal changes of urban expansion due to the influence of Guangzhou–Foshan Inter-City Rail Transit in South China. Moreover, it has been used for assessing the environmental consequences of urbanization. Dissanayake et al. [12] assessed the change in LULC in Addis Abeba City, Ethiopia during a 15-year period (1986–2016) and compared and contrasted it with changes in land surface temperature in the study area.

2.2 Urban expansion intensity index

The urban expansion intensity index (UEII) is the ratio of the change in urban land area in a unit of time to the total land area in a spatial unit. In other words, it quantifies the change in a built-up area between different given points in time as a proportion of the total area of the landscape. UEII is computed using Eq. (2), and the higher value implies fast urban expansion [13].

$$UEII = \left(\frac{\Delta A_{\Delta t}}{A_L}\right) * \frac{1}{\Delta t} \tag{2}$$

where *UEII* is the changing intensity for a given time interval (e.g., t0–t1); $\Delta A_{\Delta t}$ is the area of land change from non-built-up to built-up during the given time interval; A_L is the area of the entire landscape; and Δt is the time span of the given time interval.

UEII normalizes the mean annual expansion based on the total land area of the landscape and makes the results comparable in temporal sets [6, 14, 15]. Additionally, UEII could be employed to recognize the preferences of urban growth and to compare the speed or intensity of land use changes in a particular urban setting in a certain period.

The annual urban expansion intensity of a spatial unit can be used to compare the quantitative characteristics of urban expansion over different study periods [16]. UEII was among the key indicators used to examine urban expansion from the perspective of nonurban to urban conversion, detailing the spatiotemporal variations and impact factors of urban expansion in Qingdao [6]. It has also been applied in the identification and analysis of urban sprawl of the Tripoli metropolitan area, conducted by Al-sharif et al. [17].

2.3 Urban spatial expansion rate

The urban spatial expansion rate (USER) is an indicator based on the concept of the pace of urban development and the dynamic change in the spatial structure of a given urban region as varying in time. The rate of land-use change is critical for determining the conversion process associated with urban development and expansion [10]. USER assumes that urban growth is an exponential process (**Figure 2**) that is theoretically equivalent to the yearly rate of compound interest [14]. The formula in Eq. (3) is used to calculate the USGR.

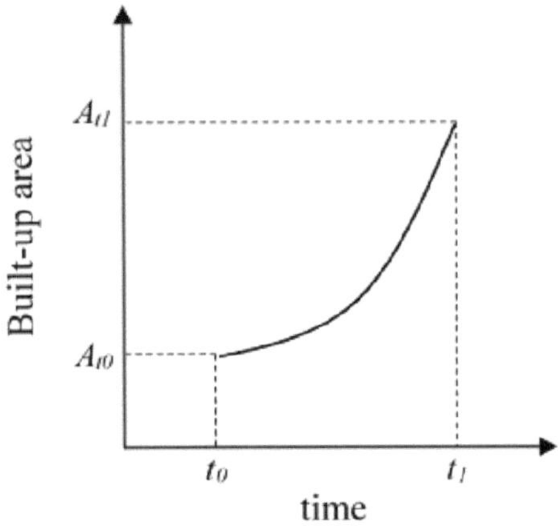

Figure 2.
Geometric change model (increments of growth increase over time, at a constant rate of increase).

$$USER = \left(\frac{A_{t1}}{A_{t0}}\right)^{\frac{1}{\Delta t}} - 1 \quad (3)$$

where A_{t0} and A_{t1} denote areas of built-up land at a time $t0$ (*initial*) and $t1$ (*final*), respectively, and Δt is the length of time from the time $t0$ to $t1$. When Δt is in a unit of a year, then *USER* is the annual rate of change in the spatial extent of built-up land.

By avoiding the size effect, USER converts urban expansion into a standard metric, which makes it more suitable for intercomparison of urban growth in different spatial zones and different years, as well as among different cities. Accordingly, it has been widely applied in various studies to compare the spatio-temporal dynamics of urban growth in several cities [9, 15, 16, 18, 19]. For instance, Terfa et al. [9] employed USER in order to compare the patterns of yearly urban growth in three Ethiopian cities: Adama, Hawassa, and Addis Abeba. Furthermore, Forget et al. [19] utilized this index to study the urban expansion of 45 Urban Areas in sub-Saharan Africa, whereas Zhao et al. [15] used USGR to assess the pace of urban expansion of 32 major Chinese cities over three decades.

2.4 Urban expansion type (UET)

The urban expansion type (UET) is a quantitative method for distinguishing between urban development typologies. The spatial link between existing urban regions and newly built components determines how urban development types are classified [7, 18]. The expansion types of newly developed urban land are classified as leapfrogging, edge expansion, and infilling (**Figure 3**). Infilling development denotes nonurban land that is surrounded by urban land that has experienced a change to built-up; edge-expansion or urban fringe development refers to newly developed urban areas that spread out from the edges of pre-growth built-up areas; leapfrogging refers to the development of a new urban patch that has no spatial connection to existing urban land. Infilling is associated with a more compact urban form, whereas edge expansion and leapfrogging lead to a more distributed urban form.

The UET is calculated using Eq. (4) and the value can range from 0 to 1. Xu et al. [20] proposed that the type of the observed growth be determined as infilling

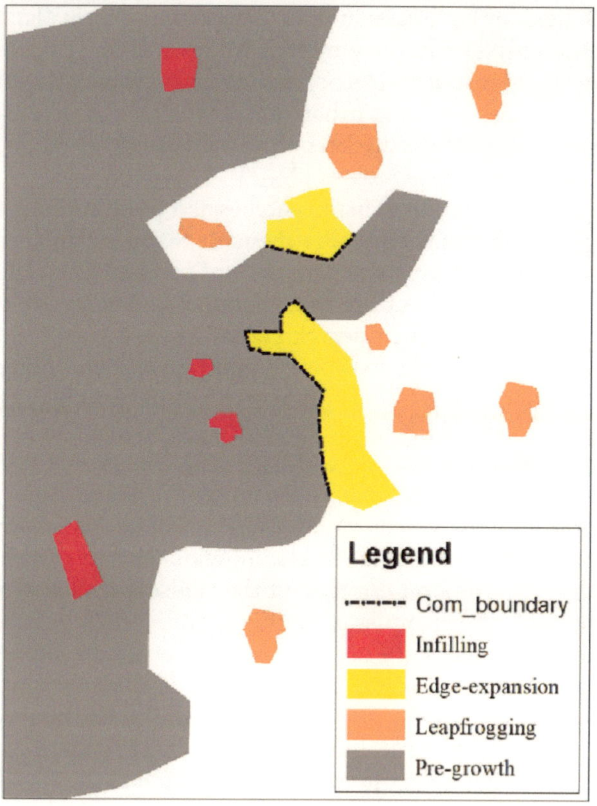

Figure 3.
Typology of urban growth.

($UET > 0.5$), edge-expansion ($0 < UET \leq 0.5$), and leapfrogging ($UET = 0$), which shows no shared boundary.

$$UET = \frac{L_{com}}{P_{new}} \tag{4}$$

where L_{com} denotes the length of the common edge between the newly developed and the pre-growth urban patches; P_{new} represents the perimeter of the new urban patches.

Among several recent studies that applied UET, Terfa et al. [9] used this index to categorize and contrast the growth types of different Ethiopian cities. Zhao et al. [15] also applied UET to determine the urban growth process of China's major cities. Moreover, this index was used in the research of Anees et al. [7], which examined the various types of growth that occurred in Srinagar city and its environs between 1999 and 2017.

2.5 Landscape metrics

The landscape metrics are quantitative indices developed to characterize and assess the landscape patterns of a specific geographic area. They are also known as spatial metrics, spatial indices, or landscape indices. Although the term "landscape metrics" has traditionally been used to describe metrics for quantifying patterns in categorical maps [21], the use of these indices has opened up a new way of describing the spatial heterogeneity of urbanized land and urban morphological characteristics in recent decades. As a result, these indices are becoming increasingly used for studying land use patterns and urban growth processes [22, 23].

Landscape indices are computed using patches as a basic building block. A patch is a spatially homogenous region with similar thematic features that are distinct from the surrounding environment. **Figure 4** depicts several patches with eight distinct land use and land cover classes. Built-up areas are commonly employed as a thematic class of interest in urban spatial pattern research [1, 24].

Landscape indices quantify the two most important aspects of landscape pattern: composition and configuration. Composition refers to the number, amount, and area of each patch type without taking into account the individual patches' spatial characteristics, placement, or location in the landscape [25]. The proportion or area of each class, as well as the number of various classes present in a landscape, are examples of composition. On the other hand, configuration denotes the spatial arrangement and distribution of the various land cover classes. Individual patch shapes (e.g., compact or sinuous) and their distribution throughout the landscape, such as whether they are aggregated or scattered, are examples of configuration.

A number of urban studies have used landscape metrics: for instance, the analysis of spatio-temporal urban dynamics in 11 smart cities in Uttar Pradesh, India [23]; a study of the growth patterns and status of urban sprawl in Chennai city's administrative boundary and areas within a 10 km buffer; and an assessment of landscape changes based on a multiple-scenario modeling approach in the Munich region [26]. Despite the fact that a number of spatial metrics have been developed and their applications are widespread, among the commonly applied indices in the quantification of urban expansion patterns in urban studies are explained below by categorizing the indices based on the potential of metric computations at three conceptual levels of analysis: patch-level, class-level, and landscape-level.

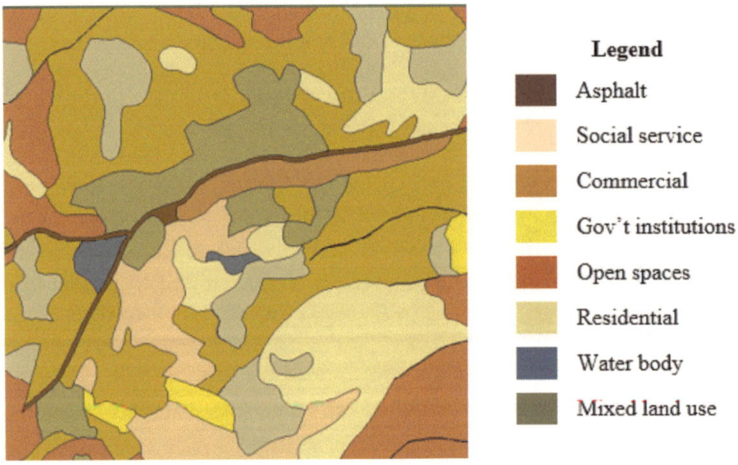

Figure 4.
Patches of different urban land use and land cover classes.

2.5.1 Patch-level indices

Patch level indices describe the spatial nature and context of individual patches and are defined for each one. Although the calculated values of each individual patch may have minimal interpretative significance in most cases, these indices are typically used as the computational basis for numerous landscape metrics, such as average patch characteristics over all patches in a class or landscape. Patch area (PA) and perimeter (PERIM) are the most useful characteristics of a particular patch. The area of each patch that makes up a landscape mosaic is perhaps the most essential and valuable piece of information contained in the landscape, as it is the basis of the patch, class, and landscape indices [21]. The range of PA is limited by the size of the landscape; in some cases, PA may be further constrained by the specification of minimum patch size. A perimeter is another fundamental piece of information available about a landscape. The perimeter of a patch is specifically regarded as an edge, and the intensity and distribution of edges are key features of landscape design. Furthermore, most indices are based on the relationship between PERIM and PA.

2.5.2 Class level-indices

The class-level indices integrate all the built-up patches. The unique configuration of patches throughout the terrain results in new aggregate attributes at the class level. The class level indices separately measure the amount and spatial arrangement of urbanized patches, allowing for a quantitative assessment of the extent and fragmentation of built-up land in the landscape. In urban studies, the most commonly used class level indices are the number of patches, mean patch size, largest path index, landscape shape index, area weighted mean patch fractal dimension, and patch cohesion index.

The *number of patches* (*NP*) represents the degree of fragmentation in built-up land; it is used to calculate the degree of disintegration of the urbanized area. Having a higher NP value indicates a dispersed distribution of patches, whereas a lower value of NP indicates a compact distribution of patches. For instance, the number of patches of the built-up area is high; it shows highly scattered settlement; segregated settlement areas with other land use and land cover classes existed in between, resulting in a higher amount of dispersed distribution of built-up patches and resulting in heterogonous distribution of the built-up area [23].

The *mean patch size* (*MPS*) is a function of the number of patches in the class and total class area (Eq. (5)), and it measures the average area of a patch in a particular class. Although MPS is derived from the number of patches, it does not convey any information about how many patches are present. A mean patch size of 5 ha could represent 1 or 100 patches.

$$MPS = \frac{\sum_{j=1}^{n} a_{ij}}{n_i} \tag{5}$$

where

$$A_{min} < MPS \leq A_{max}$$

The *largest patch index (LPI)* quantifies the percentage of landscape area occupied by the largest patch of a class (Eq. (6)).

$$LPI = \frac{Max_{a_{ij}}}{A} \tag{6}$$

where

$$0 < LPI \leq 1$$

LPI can simply be understood as a measure of the dominance of a patch in the overall landscape. Having an LPI value close to zero indicates that the corresponding patch size is becoming small, whereas a larger patch size close to 1 indicates entire landscape is dominated by a particular patch type [24].

The *Landscape shape index* (*LSI*) describes the irregularity of the complete landscape (Eq. (7)). The value of LSI indicates patch shape complexity by computing the degree of deviation, a patch has from a square or circle with an equal area [11].

$$LSI = \frac{0.25E^*}{\sqrt{A}} \tag{7}$$

where 0.25 is the square shape parameter, E^* = total length of the edge of built-up patches; A = total area of built-up land

LSI > 1, with no limit. LSI = 1 indicates that the patch has the most regular form; the higher the LSI value, the further the patch deviates from the square and the more irregular the shape.

Area weighted mean patch fractal dimension (*AWMPFD*) is a specialized landscape metric for landscape pattern analysis and its minimum and maximum values are 1 and 2, respectively [21]. It determines the overall shape and edge of urbanized land (Eq. (8)). Aggregated shapes better establish connections among various patches.

By weighing patches according to size, AWMPFD averages the fractal dimensions of all urban patches. A perimeter-area comparison is used to describe the patch's complexity and fragmentation. When a patch has a compact rectangular form with a small perimeter as compared to its area, it has a low value. At similar area sizes, more complex and fractured patches have larger perimeters, resulting in a higher fractal dimension [16].

$$AWMPFD = \sum_{i=1}^{m} \sum_{j=1}^{n} \left[\frac{2 \ln \left(0.25 P_{ij}\right)}{\ln a_{ij}} \right] \left(\frac{a_{ij}}{A} \right) \tag{8}$$

a_{ij} area of patch ij.
P_{ij} perimeter of patch ij.

2.5.3 Landscape-level indices

Landscape-level indices incorporate all patches of all classes of the entire landscape. These, like class metrics, can be combined using simple or weighted averaging, or they can reflect aggregate patch mosaic features. The pattern (i.e., configuration and composition) of the landscape mosaic is of main interest in many urban studies [9, 24, 26]. In urban studies, indices such as percentage of landscape, Patch density (PD), edge density, and mean euclidean distance neighbor are frequently used at the landscape level.

Percentage of landscape (*PLAND*) quantifies the proportional abundance of each type of patch in the landscape (Eq. (9)); i.e., the relative abundance of each urbanized part of the landscape. Because it is a relative measure, it may be a better measure of landscape composition than a class area for comparing landscapes of different sizes [23].

$$PLAND = \frac{\sum_{j=1}^{n} a_{ij}}{A} * 100 \tag{9}$$

a_{ij} is area of the jth patch of ith class.

A = total landscape area.

Patch density (*PD*) is the number of patches of a particular class per unit area (Eq. (10)), and indicates urban fragmentation; i.e., as the number of patches increases, patch density increases, representing higher fragmentation (scatter), whereas low PD reflects infilling, implying aggregation.

Patch density is a fundamental aspect of landscape pattern. It has the same basic utility as the number of patches as an index, except that it expresses the number of patches on a per unit area basis that facilitates comparisons among landscapes of varying sizes. If total landscape area is held constant, then patch density and the number of patches convey the same information. Like the number of patches, patch density often has limited interpretive value by itself because it conveys no information about the size and spatial distribution of patches.

$$PD = \frac{Number\ of\ patches}{Total\ area\ of\ the\ landscape} \tag{10}$$

Edge density (*ED*) is used to characterize the irregularity and shape complexity of urban patches (Eq. (11)).

$$ED = \frac{\sum_{k=1}^{m} e_{ik}}{A} \tag{11}$$

e_{ik} = total length of edge in landscape with patch type (class) i, including landscape boundary and patch type i background segments.

A = total landscape area.

Mean Euclidean distance Neighbor (EMN_{MN}) measures the average of the distances between the nearest patches in a class (Eq. (12)). It increases when the distance between the respective patches keeps increasing.

$$EMN_{MN} = \frac{\sum_{j=1}^{n} d_{ij}}{n_i} \tag{12}$$

where d_{ij} is the Euclidean distance between patches i and j and n_i is the total number of patches in the landscape. Range > 1 without limit.

3. Factors affecting selection of indices

Different urban expansion analysis methods are discussed in the previous section. Although these techniques have been applied in different studies, selection among the methods requires understanding of features of the techniques that are summarized in **Table 1**. On the other hand, the selection of an appropriate method of spatio-temporal analysis of urban growth can be influenced by several factors, including the purpose and objectives of the analysis, the detail of the required information, available resources, and the scale of the analysis.

Index	Strength	Limitation
Urban spatial expansion index (USEI)	• Relatively, it is simple to calculate and understand.	• Provides a constant magnitude of change over the study period/time interval considered, which may not reflect the realistic nature of urban growth. • As it can be influenced by the spatial extents of the study areas, it may not provide reliable results in the comparative assessment of the impacts of urbanization on different urban regions. • It provides limited information about the urban growth process.
Urban expansion intensity index (UEII)	• It normalizes the mean annual expansion based on the total land area of the landscape and makes the results comparable in temporal sets. • When used for different land uses in a particular urban area, it enables us to recognize the preferences of urban growth.	• In other words, because the spatial extents of the cities differ, comparing them using this index may not yield a reliable result.
Urban spatial expansion rate (USER)	• It assumes the dynamic change in the spatial structure of a given urban region varies in time, which reflects the more realistic nature of urban growth. • It avoids the size effect and is more suitable for comparative analysis between different spatial zones and different years, as well as among different cities.	• It does not provide the magnitude of expansion.
Urban expansion type (UET)	• It is a simple quantitative method to distinguish the growth types; thereby useful for identifying the types of urban form. • It is suitable to characterize the evolution process of urban expansion, and it provides a deeper understanding of the landscape transformation processes.	• It does not provide the magnitude, rate, and patterns of expansion. • Obtaining input information for computation could require more time. • The range of the values to define the growth type could be subjective, as there is no standard. • It focuses on one-dimensional (linear) properties of old and new built-up patches.
Landscape metrics	• It is suitable to assess the composition and configuration of landscapes. • It allows the analysis at different spatial scales. • It enables identification of patch expansion types. • It allows capturing the evolution process of urban expansion patterns.	• They can only quantitatively reflect the landscape patterns and their distribution for one single time period. • It is difficult to extract input information and requires special software packages for data processing • Some landscape metrics are limited interpretive value by themselves (e.g., number of patches), because they convey no information about the Area, distribution, and density of patches. • Unless the metrics are selected carefully, they could provide the same information as the landscape, as most of them are redundant and correlated.

Table 1.
Summary of features of the urban expansion analysis methods.

A particular analysis could simply aim to determine the magnitude of expansion, or it could require information on how the changes occur. In other cases, there may be a need for information about the patterns or to determine the typologies of urban expansion. The needed accuracy or level of detail in an analysis also plays an important role in selecting the methods of analysis. The requirements of information must be adapted to achieve a good balance between the time, the cost, and the quality aspects of a project.

Landscape indices, on the other hand, are based on the same fundamental measurements (i.e., amount, area, perimeter, adjacency, and distance). Indices that measure or represent the same basic information are considered conceptually redundant since they measure the same item and hence offer the same landscape information. Indices that comprise similar measures for the basic components of configuration and composition are often empirically redundant because they are statistically correlated [26]. Many indices are also scale-dependent, which means that their values vary as the scale of the input data increases (both resolution and extent). As a result, it is the researcher's responsibility to choose a collection of nonredundant metrics that are suitable for studying the situation at hand.

4. Conclusions

This chapter provided an overview of the prevailing methods of spatio-temporal analysis of built-up expansion. It presented various approaches to quantify the absolute magnitude of expansion, rate, intensity, and growth type. Moreover, landscape indices, which are devoted to determining the composition and configuration of built-up expansion, are also discussed. Each of these methods has benefits and drawbacks for applications, posing a lot of work for users to select an appropriate method for the situation at hand. In this respect, this chapter provides a good insight into the main features of existing methods and would help researchers and potential users undertake effective analysis, balancing between their needs and resource requirements.

Author details

Dejene Tesema Bulti* and Anteneh Lemmi Eshete
Adama Science and Technology University, Adama, Ethiopia

*Address all correspondence to: dejenetesema@yahoo.com

References

[1] Li S, Liu X, Li Z, Wu Z, Yan Z, Chen Y. Spatial and temporal dynamics of urban expansion along the Guangzhou – Foshan Inter-City rail transit corridor, China. Sustainablity. 2018;**10**(593):301-311

[2] Viana CM, Oliveira S, Oliveira SC, Jorge R. Land use/land cover change detection and urban sprawl analysis. In: Spatial Modeling in GIS and R for Earth and Environmental Sciences. Amsterdam, Netherlands: Elsevier Inc; 2019. pp. 621-652

[3] Dong T, Jiao L, Xu G, Yang L, Liu J. Towards sustainability ? Analyzing changing urban form patterns in the United States, Europe , and China. Science Total Environment. 2019;**671**: 632-643

[4] Kindu M, Angelova D, Schneider T, Döllerer M, Teketay D, Knoke T. Monitoring of urban growth patterns in rapidly growing Bahir Dar City of Northwest Ethiopia with 30 year Landsat imagery record. International Journal of Geo-Information. 2020:1-19

[5] Estoque RC, Murayama Y. Land Use Policy Intensity and spatial pattern of urban land changes in the megacities of Southeast Asia. Land Use Policy. 2015; **48**:213-222

[6] Qiuying L, Chuanglin F, Guangdong L, Zhoupeng R. Quantitative measurement of urban expansion and its driving factors in Qingdao: An Empirical Analysis Based on County Unit Data. 2015;**6**(3):172-179

[7] Anees MM, Mann D, Sharma M, Banzhaf E. Assessment of urban dynamics to understand spatiotemporal Di ff erentiation at various scales using remote sensing and geospatial tools. Remote Sensing. 2020; **12**(1306)

[8] Li H, Hua Y, Wei D, Huang Z. Urban land expansion and spatial dynamics in globalizing Shanghai. Sustainability. 2014:8856-8875

[9] Terfa BK, Chen N, Liu D, Zhang X, Niyogi D. Urban expansion in Ethiopia from 1987 to 2017: Characteristics, spatial patterns, and driving forces. Sustainablity. 2019;**11** (2973):1-21

[10] Dutta D, Rahman A, Paul SK, Kundu A. Estimating urban growth in peri-urban areas and its interrelationships with built-up density using earth observation datasets. Annals of Regional Science. 2020. DOI: 10.1007/s00168-020-00974-8

[11] Liu Y, Zuo R, Dong Y. Analysis of temporal and Spatial characteristics of urban expansion in Xiaonan District from 1990 to 2020 Using Time Series Landsat Imagery. 2021

[12] Dissanayake D, Morimoto T, Murayama Y, Ranagalage M. Impact of landscape structure on the variation of land surface temperature in Sub-Saharan Region: A case Study of Addis Ababa using Landsat Data. 2016

[13] Sun Y, Zhao S, Qu W. Quantifying spatiotemporal patterns of urban expansion in three capital cities in Northeast China over the past three decades using satellite data sets. Environmental Earth Science. 2014. DOI: 10.1007/s12665-014-3901-6

[14] Li C, Li J, Wu J. Quantifying the speed, growth modes, and landscape pattern changes of urbanization: A

hierarchical patch dynamics approach. Landscape Ecology. 2013:1875-1888

[15] Zhao S, Zhou D, Zhu C, Qu W, Zhao J, Sun Y. Rates and patterns of urban expansion in China's 32 major cities over the past three decades. Landscape Ecology. 2015. DOI: 10.1007/s10980-015-0211-7

[16] Xu X, Min X. Quantifying spatiotemporal patterns of urban expansion in China using remote sensing data. Cities. 2013;**35**:104-113

[17] Al-sharif AAA, Pradhan B, Shafri HZM, Mansor S. Quantitative analysis of urban sprawl in Tripoli using Pearson' s Chi-Square statistics and urban expansion intensity index. In: 7th IGRSM International Remote Sensing & GIS Conference and Exhibition. IOP Conf. Series: Earth and Environmental Science. 2014;**20**:012006

[18] Sun Y, Zhao S. Spatiotemporal dynamics of urban expansion in 13 cities across the Jing-Jin-Ji Urban Agglomeration from 1978 to 2015. Ecological Indicators. 2018;**87**:302-313

[19] Forget Y, Shimoni M, Gilbert M. Mapping 20 years of urban expansion in 45 urban areas of sub-Saharan Africa. Remote Sensing. 2021;**2021**:1-19

[20] Xu C, Liu M, Zhang C, An S, Yu W, Chen JM. The spatiotemporal dynamics of rapid urban growth in the Nanjing metropolitan region of China the spatiotemporal dynamics of rapid urban growth in the Nanjing metropolitan region of China. Landscape Ecology. 2007;**22**:925-937

[21] Mcgarigal K. FRAGSTATS HELP. 2015

[22] Manesha EPP, Jayasinghe A, Nawod H. Measuring urban sprawl of small and medium towns using GIS and remote sensing techniques : A case study of Sri Lanka. Egyptian Journal of Remote Sensing. 2021. DOI: 10.1016/j.ejrs.2021.11.001

[23] Aithal BH, Ramachandra TV. Visualization of urban growth pattern in Chennai using geoinformatics and Spatial metrics. Journal of the Indian Society of Remote Sensing. 2016;**44**(4):617-633

[24] Verma R, Garg PK. Analysis of spatio-temporal urban dynamics in 11 smart cities of analysis of spatio-temporal urban dynamics in 11 smart cities. International Architectural Photogrammetric Remote Sensing Spatial Information Sciences. 2021;**XLVI**:557-564

[25] Sapena M, Ruiz LÁ. Analysis of land use / land cover spatio-temporal metrics and population dynamics for urban growth characterization. Computational Environmental Urban System. 2018;**2018**:1

[26] Xu C, Haase D, Su M, Wang Y, Pauleit S. Assessment of landscape changes under different urban dynamics based on a multiple-scenario modeling approach. Urban Analytical City Science. 2020:1-19. DOI: 10.1177/2399808320910161

Section 3

Policy Decisions

Chapter 5

Linking Land Use Changes to Policy Decisions: The Case of Northeastern Iran

Mehdi Sarparast and Maryam Niknejad

Abstract

Land use change is the most important cause of disturbances in the natural environment. It increases the severity of natural disasters such as floods, dust storms, etc. Moreover, it also leads to major unnatural events such as water, soil, and air pollution and land subsidence. Land use change can take many forms in different parts of the world. The vast majority of these changes are the result of erroneous and unscientific policies that may be beneficial in the short term, but have negative long-term impact on human societies and the environment. Wrong policies lead to erroneous and short-term development and, in the long run, irreversible socioeconomic and environmental challenges. In this chapter, the process of land use change, driving forces (political decisions, technological development, etc.), causes, and effects of changes were all considered in a socio-ecological system in northeastern Iran (As a representative of the hyper-arid, arid, and semiarid regions of Iran). The discussion is captured in a framework reflecting driving forces, pressures, state of affairs, responses, and impacts (DPSIR framework).

Keywords: land use change, policymakers' decisions

1. Introduction

Land use change is an important cause of disturbance in the natural environment as it increases the severity of natural disasters such as floods, dust storms, etc. It also causes significant unnatural events such as water, soil, and air pollution, land subsidence, and eventually, desertification [1]. Land cover changes occur naturally over time but are hastened by human activity. Land use and land cover changes have accelerated over the last three centuries, owing largely to the impact of technological advances associated with the Industrial Revolution. It is estimated that between 1950 and 1980, more forests were cleared than between the early eighteenth and nineteenth centuries combined. While forest cover has decreased by 20% since 1700, cropland areas have more than quadrupled [2].

Land use change can take many forms in different parts of the world, ranging from such factors as urbanization [3], deforestation [4], farming, overgrazing, and hydraulic terraces [5], coastal wind farm development [6], and mining [7]. The vast majority of these factors emanate from erroneous and unscientific policies that may be beneficial in the short term, but have a negative long-term impact on human societies and the environment. Wrong policies lead to erroneous and short-term development and, in the long run, irreversible socioeconomic and environmental challenges. Land use activities in developing countries, on the other hand, accelerated primarily during the twentieth century and continue to this day [8]. These countries are attempting to boost agricultural output while depleting their natural resource base. Over the last 50 years, most regions in Iran have continued to expand and intensify their land use activities [8]. Deforestation and agricultural expansion have been the dominant patterns of land cover change over the last five centuries [5]. Changes in land use practices, such as agricultural land management and urbanization, have, however, been significant drivers of change. In this chapter, the process of land use change, driving forces, or causes and effects of changes in northeastern Iran for two time periods (1977–2001, 2001–2016) are discussed.

2. Materials and methods

2.1 Study area description

Iran, with a population of 85 million people, is located in arid and semiarid regions of the world, and farming accounts for more than 30% of the people's income. The study sites are Taybad-Bakharz is an arid and semiarid region of Iran's Razavi Khorasan province (**Figure 1**). Taybad-Bakharz encompassed an area of 4800 km^2, with a current population of 160,000 people. Over 70% of rural people's income

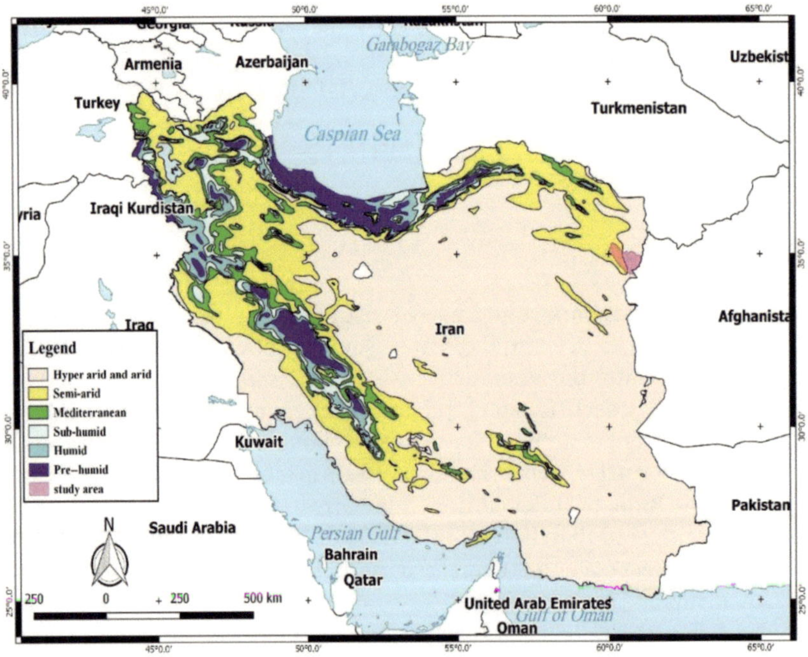

Figure 1.
The study area's location, as well as the spatial distribution of climatic zones in Iran.

comes from livestock, with the remaining 30% coming from farming. Precipitation ranges from 100 to 260 mm, with desert border areas receiving less. Rainfall varies greatly in both time and space. The average yearly temperature is around 16°C, but during the summer, the temperature can reach 42°C. In addition, annual potential evapotranspiration (PET) ranges from 800 to 2000 mm. Wind speeds range from 5.3 to 6.8 m/s, with the highest recorded in May at around 6 m/s. Furthermore, wind blows over 120 days per year [8, 9].

2.2 Factors influencing land use change in the DPSIR framework

Taybad-Bakharz region has experienced population growth over the last 50 years. This region currently has a total resident population of 160,000. Fifty percent of the population lives in rural areas and relies entirely on agriculture and animal husbandry for a living. Qanats used to provide water for agriculture and animal husbandry. However, since 1960, this region has undergone a significant transformation due to technological advancement and the arrival of the drilling industry, as well as Land Reform Law (the division of land among farmers), with a large portion of rangeland converted to agriculture. The Environmental European Agency's DPSIR (Driving force-Pressure-State-Impacts-Responses) framework was used to categorize effective information and identify a set of key indicators to better describe land use change, relationships, and feedback between factors. The PRESSURE indicators are associated with the hazardous effects tolerated by the environment under various types of pressure (physical, human, etc.). The understanding of pressures necessitates the estimation of determinant factors. DRIVING FORCES generate these indicators. This indicator category represents anthropogenic activities and the various processes that have an impact on land use change. They provide a general indication of the causes of changes in land use. In any case, they are primarily indicators of human activities such as intensive agricultural practices, overgrazing, population growth, tourism expansion, and so on. The IMPACT indicators describe the consequences of land use change, both onsite (soil loss, poverty, etc.) and offsite (flooding). The RESPONSE indicators are linked to the corrective actions taken to improve the STATE and lower the PRESSURES that influence it. These types of indicators are useful in land use change protection programs. They are in charge of "measuring" the actions and policies used to mitigate human pressures and other factors that contribute to the process of land use change.

2.3 Land use and land cover data

Initially, Landsat satellite imagery for the years 1977, 2001, and 2016 was downloaded from https://earthexplorer.usgs.gov using the following criteria (**Table 1**).

Year Produced	Satellite type	Image Date	WRS Path/ Row	Spatial Resolution	sensor
1977	Landsat3	13 May	158/36	60 m	MSS
2001	Landsat4	13 May	158/36	30 m	TM
2016	Landsat8	25 May	158/36	30 m	OLI and TIRS

Table 1.
Data type and technical properties of satellite images used in this study.

The quality of satellite images was then examined for geometric and radiometric errors such as striping, Atmospheric Interference, skewing on Scanline, and projection distortion. To accurately identify the Earth's surface condition, a false color composite (bands 7,4,1) was created for each satellite image [10]. A land use map was created for three different times to investigate changes in land use/land cover (1977, 2001, and 2016). The supervised classification method/maximum likelihood algorithm (using all spectral bands except the sixth band) was used to create the final land use maps. Topographic maps from the National Cartographic Agency (at a scale of l: 25000), aerial photographs at a scale of 1:20000, and regional land use maps were used for this purpose.

Groundwater depletion (GWD), electrical conductivity (EC), total dissolved solids (TDS), acidity (pH), and sodium adsorption ratio (SAR) parameters were used to assess groundwater changes over two time periods. The methods for calculating the aforementioned criteria are detailed in the following link: DOI: 10.1016/j.rsase.2020.100348

3. Results and discussion

3.1 Land use changes

Land use maps for 1977, 2001, and 2016 were obtained using Landsat satellite images, as shown in **Figure 2**. Given the maps, the study area's land uses were classified into five categories: (1) residential area, (2) cropland, (3) salty land, (4) rangeland, and (5) barren land. According to the findings, barren lands and rangeland had the highest percentage of area in 1977, accounting for 85.5% of the total area. In 2001, this percentage remained nearly constant, with a 10% decrease in the rangelands. In 2016, there are no significant changes, and this proportion is similar to that of 2001. The greatest

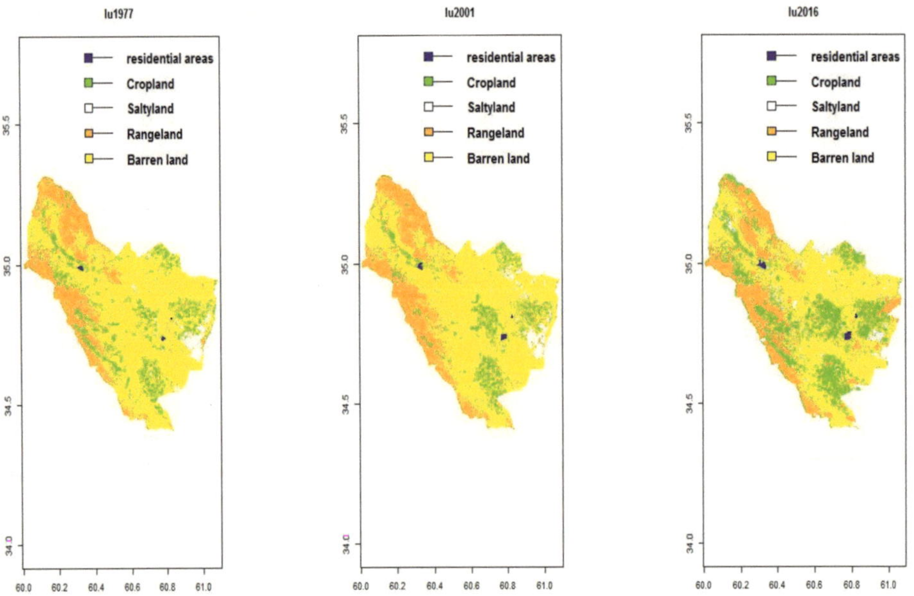

Figure 2.
Maps of land use changes.

percentage of change in barren lands and rangeland occurred between 1977 and 2001. The area of salty land remained constant over two periods, with a slight change in the second. This land use accounts for 6.5% of the total area. The proportion of irrigated and rain-fed agricultural lands increased in both time phases with 2 and 5% of growth during the first and the second phases, respectively. In fact, the percentage of agricultural areas experienced a steady rise from 7.8% in 1977 to 9.7% in 2001 and 14.3% in 2016. Due to the continuous growth in the population from 50,000 people in 1977 to 160,000 people in 2016, the growth of the residential area growth was dynamic during the two time phases with huge rise from 0.14 to 0.4% (**Figure 2**). The portion of rangeland areas decreased steadily from 42.7 (1977) to 32.2% (2001), and 29.3% (2016).

During these times, 288 deep and semi-deep wells were drilled in the area. These developments, combined with poor management of groundwater discharge, resulted in the cultivation of a large portion of rangeland. Given that barren lands had no productivity, and this land use included badlands, salty land, and rocky surfaces. Then, much of the rangeland was converted to agriculture. Most Qanats had dried. Because of these circumstances, the government and people were encouraged to drill deep wells to supply water for drinking, agriculture, and animal husbandry. As a result of these practices, agriculture reached its peak in 2016. Crops such as melons, wheat, barley, sugar beet, cotton, and crocus (saffron) were produced on a large scale as agricultural levels increased. This increase in production resulted in a decrease in groundwater level (**Figure 3**), so that the southern half of the region experienced 1.5-meter depletion per year during the second period.

Due to the close proximity of fresh and saltwater aquifers in this area, a sharp annual depletion, and high evapotranspiration, the possibility of displacement in the fresh and saltwater boundary is very high. As a result, some freshwater wells have been completely salted, and agricultural activities have been discontinued. This approximate displacement is irreversible. TDS and EC are increasing in the region's south. This movement is toward areas with the greatest water depletion.

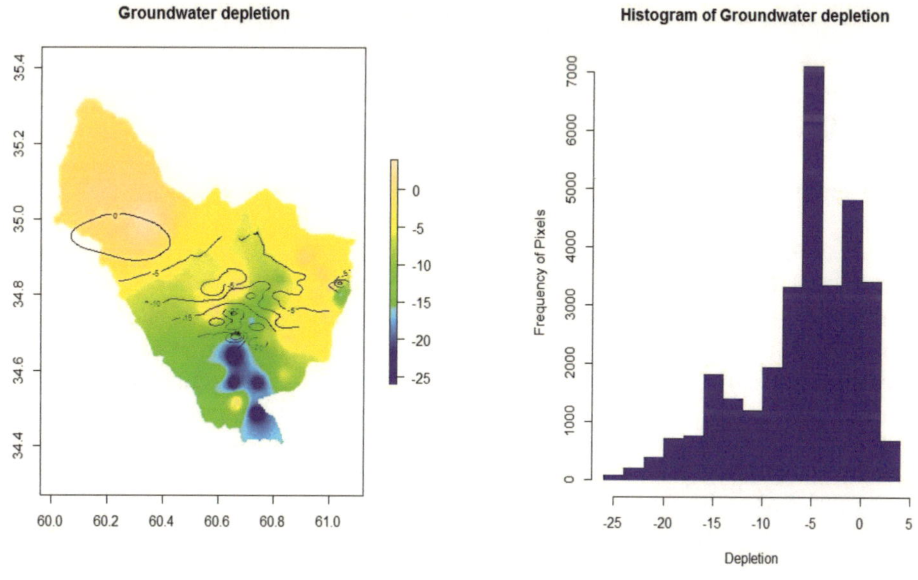

Figure 3.
Groundwater depletion.

Given that land use changes occurred at their peak, the most significant changes in this region will be an increase in residential areas. And this change is occurring in urban areas. It is predicted that as rural incomes decline and people lose their jobs, villages will become haunted and migration will begin.

It is obvious that a significant land use change has occurred in the Taybad-Bakharz region. Capable lands were converted to agricultural lands over a 40-year period (**Figure 2**). Technology and agricultural machinery entry, deep well drilling industry, and wet years that encouraged people to cultivate lands are three important factors that lead to increased agriculture areas. Currently, irrigated agriculture has reached its maximum potential and is entirely dependent on water discharge. Furthermore, farming and crop activities provide a living for many families. In recent years, regional management actions have been able to control discharge, digging wells, and land use conversion to some extent. However, these management practices have not been successful because aquifers have been depleted for many years, increasing the possibility of a disruption in people's livelihood conditions as precipitation decreases and aquifer recharge continues. Unless comprehensive management actions are taken at the local and regional levels, agricultural growth in the Taybad-Bakharz region is expected to slow and eventually stop, resulting in bare lands and dust storms. Due to ineffective policies in the past, the livelihoods of a large portion of the region's population have become dependent on agriculture, resulting in increased ground water extraction. The dependent population will be jeopardized as groundwater levels fall and salinity rises. To overcome the human-environmental catastrophe, policy-makers must develop alternative livelihoods at the regional level. Furthermore, the process of rehabilitating destroyed rangeland must be considered as soon as possible. Plowing poor rangelands in wet years should be prohibited because these lands can be a major source of dust in dry years. Furthermore, groundwater extraction should be minimized, and control policies should be tightened to reduce the severity of the risk.

3.2 DPSIR framework

The results of the case study in northeastern Iran are applicable to the Iran. The DPSIR framework was used to categorize effective information and identify a set of key indicators to better describe land use change, relationships, and feedback between factors (**Figure 4**).

3.2.1 Driving forces

Iran has changed over the years since 1960 as a result of population growth, technological development, and the Land Reform Law (the division of land between farmers). Population growth creates motivation for change. Water, food, and a place to live are just a few examples of basic human needs that can only be met by manipulating nature. Previously, the Iranian people were supplied with water via rivers, springs, Qanats, and rainwater. The traditional water supply could no longer meet the needs of the people as the urban population grew. The pattern of irrigation changed as land was fragmented. These cases were accompanied by technological and agricultural machinery advancements, resulting in abrupt changes in rangelands areas. During these periods, a large number of deep and semi-deep wells drilled.

These developments, along with mismanagement in groundwater discharge, led to a wide part of rangelands being placed under cultivation process. Then a large part

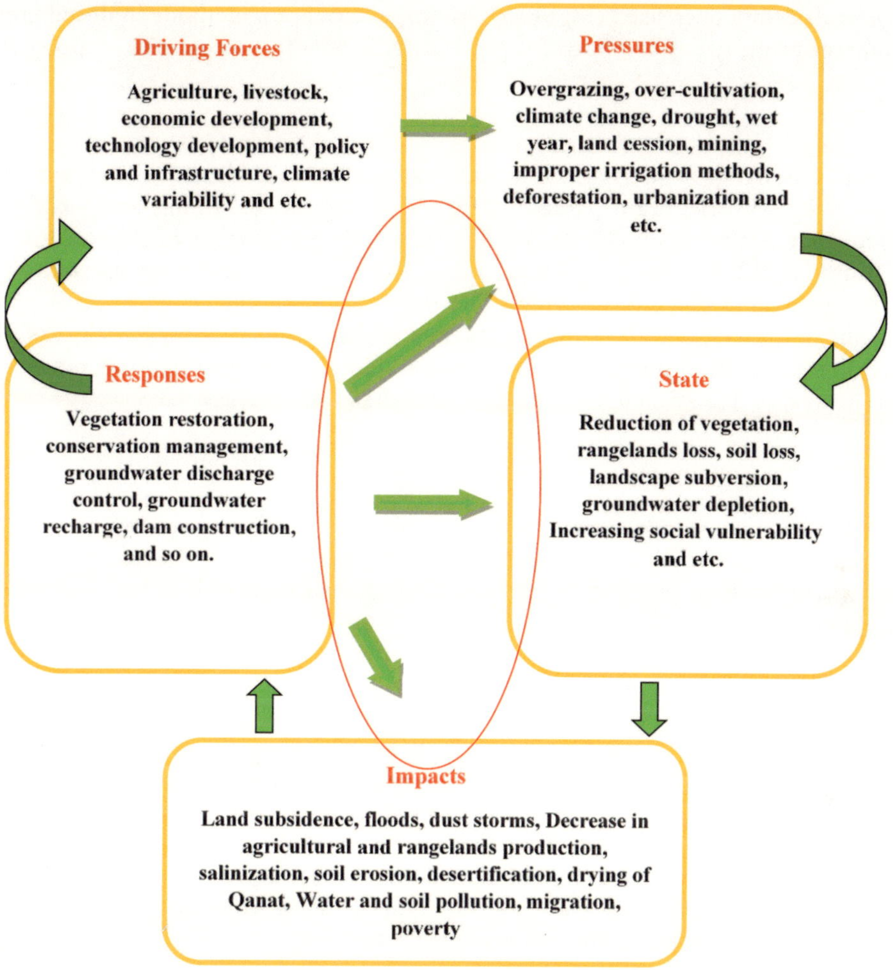

Figure 4.
DPSIR framework.

of the rangelands converted to the agriculture. Qanats dried in most areas. These circumstances encouraged the government and people to drill deep wells to supply water for the purposes of drinking, agriculture, and animal husbandry. These practices resulted in higher agriculture productivity. This increase in productivity has resulted in a decrease in groundwater levels, which are higher in arid and semiarid regions. Climate variability has also exacerbated the situation.

3.2.2 Pressures

The development of advanced agricultural machinery increased the amount of agricultural land available [8, 9]. Furthermore, during wet years, people are more likely to cultivate. Land cession policies, on the other hand, reduced the area of rangelands even further. Mining, industrial estates, and small industrial and agricultural units were all examples of land cession. These factors contribute to deforestation and the loss of rangelands. As a result, the phenomenon of overgrazing manifests itself. Overgrazing resulted from livestock concentration on a smaller area of land as the rangelands extent decreased (**Figure 3**). Improper irrigation methods (reduced crop and forage production) compound this pressure, as does the occurrence of drought.

3.2.3 State

Land use change begins in the rangelands as vegetation declines. Soil erosion starts, and soil nutrients are gradually depleted. Overgrazing, mining, and other cession activities are gradually causing landscape subversion (**Figure 5**). In addition, the shift in livelihood and complete reliance on agriculture based on groundwater discharge has created a shaky and unstable environment for human societies. Droughts, a lack of groundwater recharge, and declining groundwater levels expose the vulnerable socioeconomic system to destruction. On the other hand, as rangelands area shrinks, so do social conflicts among ranchers.

3.2.4 Impacts

Desertification, floods, dust storms, water scarcity and Qanats drying, air pollution, soil and water pollution, soil erosion, salinization, and the destruction of human communities, poverty, and migration are all examples of how land use change manifests itself.

3.2.5 Responses

There has been no positive response from policymakers in the face of widespread land use change. Until environmental disasters occur, policymakers will be unaware of the changes. Furthermore, the majority of responses concern when the environmental hazard occurred. When a flood occurs, for example, dam construction is proposed and implemented as part of a plan. Of course, programs such as vegetation restoration, groundwater management, and so on are proposed, but they are unfeasible due to a lack of water resources and a high reliance on local communities' livelihoods.

3.3 Policy decisions

Policymakers have made a variety of decisions over the years. The common denominator in these decisions is a lack of foresight. Paying attention to cross-sectional incomes while depleting non-renewable or low-renewable natural resources, regardless of the long-term outlook, has resulted in a failure situation. The first cause of the current crisis is embarrassment in technology entry and the implementation of inconsistent programs. The first blunder was digging deep wells and extracting groundwater, resulting in large dependent and vulnerable populations. Groundwater-based agriculture was a poor management decision in a country with arid and semiarid climates. The plains and hills were plowed as much as possible, so there was no plow able surface due to the slope and rocky conditions. Agricultural expansion, as well as land cessions for mining, military, sports, urban planning and settlement activities, parks, and other uses, gradually reduced the area of rangelands.

After agricultural development, mining is the most important factor in land use change, which is currently occurring at a rapid pace in high-quality rangelands. Mining activities are upturning the landscape in mountainous and steep rangelands where plowing is impossible. Heavy metal contamination in mineral residues quickly

Figure 5.
a: cultivation, b: mining, c: overgrazing (Source: Sarparast, M. (Photographer) (2022, April 20).

enters the soil and water, and over time, the energy cycle and animal and plant communities undergo changes and heterogeneity.

Agriculture expansion, mining, and other land cession have significantly reduced rangelands area. As a result, the number of livestock available is constrained to a smaller geographical area. As a consequence, overgrazing occurs, and the rangeland's tendency becomes extremely negative. However, it is always incorrect to believe that increased livestock numbers have resulted in overgrazing and rangelands destruction. Policymakers have created two vulnerable social groups in agriculture and animal husbandry by establishing cross-cutting and finite incomes with no regard for sustainable development. Unsustainable agriculture will result from declining groundwater levels, climate change (global warming), and climate variability (drought). Land use change is a multidimensional phenomenon with synergistic effects that eventually leads to environmental challenges such as desertification, land subsidence, floods, and dust storms, among others. Furthermore, a long-term drought, such as the one that occurred in the Southern Plains region of the United States in the 1930s (Dust Bowl), will result in extreme poverty and migration.

4. Future scenarios of land use change and management practices

The impact of human activities on the land has grown exponentially, changing entire landscapes, affecting soils, hydrological cycles, and climate, and in some cases leading to land use change. A variety of economic, technological, institutional, cultural, and demographic factors can be identified as the underlying driving forces of land use changes. Currently, in Iran, the process of land use change, particularly agricultural expansion, is at its peak, and environmental-human challenges are arising as a result of these changes. However, the wrong policies of plundering natural resources are causing a large, silent, and devastating change. This significant shift is the result of land cession to the mining industry. This industry exists despite the impact of topography on nature, landscape beauty, wildlife, and high-quality forage, among other things. Despite the enormous income generated by mining, no portion is distributed to local communities. This is regardless of the fact that the pastoralists have lost their pastures. This increases the vulnerability of local communities.

Management actions should be taken in two dimensions in response to land use changes:

1. Increasing policymakers' environmental knowledge and awareness

   Most management issues regard education and promotion among local communities as a means of reducing environmental damage. Meanwhile, local communities are open to all policymakers' decisions. Education and promotion among policymakers in developing countries, such as Iran, should be considered an immediate response to reducing environmental and human hazard. Because many of today's environmental challenges are the result of policymakers' lack of knowledge and awareness of environmental issues, as well as their poor decision-making. There should be two levels of training:

   A: Organizing courses and workshops for policymakers.

   B: Teaching environmental knowledge courses to university students from all fields of study who will be future policymakers.

   If training at these two levels is done properly, the conditions for sustainable development will be created. All humans on Earth require knowledge of water, soil, vegetation, and wildlife. This knowledge assists them in adapting their behavior to the environment. As a result, the life cycle is preserved, and man, as a component of the cycle, ensures his survival as well as the stability of the cycle's other components.

2. Identifying alternative livelihood opportunities to reduce local communities' vulnerability.

The next issue that requires immediate attention is reducing local communities' vulnerability by identifying alternative livelihood opportunities. Other uses, such as ecotourism, medicinal plants, sports activities, and so on, can be defined in addition to grazing livestock in rangelands. If ranchers are viewed as the primary stakeholders in the aforementioned uses, grazing pressure will decrease over time.

Author details

Mehdi Sarparast[1*] and Maryam Niknejad[2]

1 Natural Resources-Combating Desertification, Gorgan University of Agricultural Sciences and Natural Resources, Gorgan, Golestan, Iran

2 Natural Resources-Forest Science, Sari University of Agricultural Sciences and Natural Resources, Sari, Mazandaran, Iran

*Address all correspondence to: mehdisarparast@gmail.com

References

[1] Sarparast M, Ownegh M, Najafinejad A, Sepehr A. An applied statistical method to identify desertification indicators in northeastern Iran. Geoenvironmental Disasters. 2018;**5**(1):3. DOI: 10.1186/s40677-018-0095-3

[2] Klein Goldewijk K. Estimating global land use change over the past 300 years: The HYDE database. Global Biogeochemical Cycles. 2001;15(2): 417-433. [Geo-referenced global population and land use tables and maps over the last three centuries, Available from: http://www.rivm.nl/env/int/hyde]

[3] Peng J, Liu Y, Li T, Wu J. Regional ecosystem health response to rural land use change: A case study in Lijiang City, China. Ecological Indicators. 2017;**72**:399-410. DOI: 10.1016/j.ecolind.2016.08.024

[4] Islam K, Jashimuddin M, Nath B, Nath TK. Land use classification and change detection by using multi-temporal remotely sensed imagery: The case of Chunati wildlife sanctuary Bangladesh. The Egyptian Journal of Remote Sensing and Space Science. 2017;**21**:37-47. DOI: 10.1016/j.ejrs.2016.12.005

[5] Fuchs R, Herold M, Verburg PH, Clevers JGPW. A high-resolution and harmonized model approach for reconstructing and analysing historic land changes in Europe. Biogeosciences. 2013;**10**:1543-1559. DOI: 10.5194/bg-10-1543-2013

[6] Harvey N, Dew REC, Hender S. Rapid land use change by coastal wind farm development: Australian policies, politics and planning. Land Use Policy. 2017;**61**:368-378. DOI: 10.1016/j.landusepol.2016.11.031

[7] Redondo-Vega JM, Gómez-Villar A, Santos-González J, González-Gutiérrez RB, Álvarez-Martínez J. Changes in land use due to mining in the north-western mountains of Spain during the previous 50 years. Catena. 2017;**149**(3):844-856. DOI: 10.1016/j.catena.2016.03.017

[8] Sarparast M, Ownegh M, Sepehr A. Investigation the driving forces of land-use change in northeastern Iran: Causes and effects. Remote Sensing Applications: Society and Environment. 2020b;**19**:100348. DOI: 10.1016/j.rsase.2020.100348

[9] Sarparast M, Ownegh M, Sepehr A. Evaluating the impacts of combating-action programs on desertification hazard trends: A case study of Taybad-Bakharz region, northeastern Iran. Environmental and Sustainability Indicators. 2020a;**7**:100043. DOI: 10.1016/j.indic.2020.100043

[10] Khoi DD, Murayama Y. Forecasting areas vulnerable to forest conversion in the tam Dao National Park region, Vietnam. Remote Sensing. 2010;**2**(5):1249-1272. DOI: 10.3390/rs2051249